If Not Now

Developmental Readers in the College Classroom

Jeanne Henry

Boynton/Cook
HEINEMANN
Portsmouth, NH

Boynton/Cook Publishers, Inc.
A subsidiary of Reed Elsevier Inc.
361 Hanover Street
Portsmouth, NH 03801-3912

Offices and agents throughout the world

© 1995 by Jeanne Henry

Library of Congress Cataloging-in-Publication Data
Henry, Jeanne, 1960–
     If not now : developmental readers in the college classroom /
Jeanne Henry.
          p.   cm.
     Includes bibliographical references (p.   ).
     ISBN 0-86709-364-1 (alk. paper)
     1. Reading (Higher education)—United States. 2. Fiction—20th
century—Study and teaching (Higher)—United States.   I. Title.
LB2365.R4H46   1995
428.4'071'1—dc20   95-19415
                                                              CIP

Editor: Carolyn Coman
Production: Renée M. Nicholls
Copy Editor: Alan Huisman
Cover Designer: Studio Nine
Photo for Chapter 2 taken by Joe Ruh, courtesy of Northern Kentucky
University. Additional photos by Paul Ellis.

Printed in the United States of America on acid-free paper.
99 98 97 96 95 DA 1 2 3 4 5

In memory of
Al Fritz
May 8, 1925 – January 16, 1995
My friend and teacher Linda Amspaugh's
dearest friend and teacher

Contents

Acknowledgments   vii

Foreword by Thomas Newkirk   ix

Preface   xiii

CHAPTER 1:   The Road to Reading   1

CHAPTER 2:   The View from Here   15

CHAPTER 3:   Reading Workshop   25

CHAPTER 4:   Buckets O' Blood   47

CHAPTER 5:   Literary Letters   75

CHAPTER 6:   Dirty Laundry   109

CHAPTER 7:   Decision Time   133

Appendix A   142

Appendix B   146

Appendix C   148

Bibliography   153

Acknowledgments

*I*n the chapters ahead, you'll meet the students of LAP 091-04. Without them, there would be no book. In preparing this manuscript for publication, I contacted these students I taught five years ago to ask their permission to use their literary letters for commercial publication. Several graduated from Northern Kentucky University or other institutions with BAs. A few completed associate degrees and wanted to talk about furthering their education yet again. Some have married, some have new children, and some are still living at home. A couple recommended books I ought to read. They are still struggling to get ahead, but sound so much more sure of themselves than they did five years ago. They wished me well, and I wish them well in return.

You'll also meet the members of my doctoral committee at the University of Cincinnati. I think you'll conclude, as I have, that this book rests on their guidance, as well as on their willingness to see me explore an unconventional research design. They are Linda Amspaugh, chair, Chet Laine, Pat O'Reilly, and Mary Anne Pitman. I also want to thank two former UC faculty members, Karin Dahl and Vickie Purcell-Gates, who introduced me to a few right ideas at the right time. Jennifer Hiatt, a fellow doctoral student at UC and a great friend, was ready with whatever I needed, whenever.

At Northern Kentucky University, dozens of reading and writing workshops have been conducted by the following colleagues: Wanda Crawford, Paul Ellis, Patty Fairbanks, Barbara Hedges, Linda Mauser, Joan Pearon, Mary Ann Weiss, Fran Zaniello, and Karl Zuelke (along with former NKU faculty member Evieanne Timmons). Each has added his or her own spin to the workshop, and together we continue to improve our courses, our teaching, and our program. All of us owe a great debt to Jeannine Holtz, program secretary, who keeps the show on the road.

Michelle Robinson, my student assistant, has kept me laughing for the past two years. She was also the first person to read this book, since she had to photocopy it. Emily Werrell, a friend *and* an NKU reference librarian, was my ace in the hole throughout graduate school. Many thanks as well to Peg Griffin, who was neighborly enough to share everything from M&Ms to a fax machine with me. I am also grateful to Michael Ginsberg, of Jefferson Community College in Louisville, and Carolyn Coman, of Heinemann-Boynton/Cook, who are responsible for the publication of this book.

Teaching is the thing to do in my family, and I want to thank my mother, Juanita Henry, a reading and writing teacher in Texas, and my father, John P. Henry, for getting so many of us into the business. Love and thanks to Patrick, Kathy, David, and Sean Henry, as well. I don't even know how to describe the intangible help of friends like Lisa Sommer and Susan Schein, but it has something to do with skiing, taking things in stride, and the shape of things to come.

Foreword

A true story.

When I was teaching high school at Boston Trade in the early seventies, I had a great group of tenth-grade future electricians. Like many of the students at Trade, they were aliterate—they could read, but reading was not something they chose to do. So I managed to get control of the book budget and began buying books by S. E. Hinton and Gordon Parks and Paul Zindel, anything to break the stalemate that reading had become for these kids.

One day, there was a riot at the school. A group of the students (if I can use that term) ran through the halls, pounding on lockers and yelling "Strike!" Most of the school population was only too ready to acquiesce, and classes emptied. The principal ran from class to class, trying to stem the flood, but students poured out.

Except for my electricians. They sat reading S. E. Hinton and Gordon Parks and Paul Zindel. They had settled into what Jeanne Henry calls one of "the most beautiful silences on earth." I was so proud—of them, of me, of literature. The principal came to my room, glared, and said, "Mr. Newkirk, will you begin teaching."

The story rankles, even two decades later. But clearly this principal had a vision of what it meant to teach and learn—not a theory, but a clear mental image of what should be going on. If I had been at the blackboard, that would have been okay. If the students had been writing, that would have been okay. If they'd been listening to me—or even pretending to listen—that would have been okay. But simply to let them read during class, how was that instruction?

This book is about changing the mental picture of learning to read in college. Even the photographs the author includes

try to do that. Jeanne Henry sees her students as caught between two unproductive images of reading instruction. One
comes from the direct-instruction/skill-drill-and-test empire
that still flourishes within the reading profession and among
publishers who help sustain the International Reading Asso-
ciation. Reading is treated as a skill with a virtually infinite
number of isolated subskills that can be taught in isolation.
The texts and passages students read are often dull and
contrived—what Jerome Harste calls "textoids." Reading is
not a humanly motivated purposeful act but an enactment of
skills. Henry argues that this type of reading is "inauthentic"
because it ignores the reasons for which we read.

On the other front, Henry must deal with an image of
reading that comes from English departments. As an inhabit-
ant of an English department I sometimes hear the lament,
"Stephen King. Stephen King. What should we do about
Stephen King?" What should we do about this heathen in
our midst, this not even middlebrow? Henry's answer is that
we should erect statues to him—and to other writers who
keep reading alive among a wide reading public. Dean
Koontz. Anne Rice. John Grisham. Michael Crichton. Jude
Devereaux. And more. This is an honor roll of authors who
can turn nonreaders into readers.

Henry teaches at Northern Kentucky University, a place
she describes in ironic detail:

> The buildings on campus are constructed of poured concrete,
> with jutting facades, little color, few windows, and sharp techno-
> cratic angles. They form a futuristic and formidable circle of
> stone atop a hill. The first time I saw the campus, it put me in
> mind of a maximum security prison. I later learned that a folk
> legend circulating among students was the buildings were built
> to double as a prison, should the university fail.

The question, then, is which will it be for her students? Previous schooling has left many of them with negative attitudes
about education and reading. Henry finds that almost half

never read for pleasure—and almost a third agree with the statement "I feel hostility toward people who read a lot."

To turn the situation around, in her words to "give reading a second chance," Henry adopts Nancie Atwell's reading workshop approach; she asks her students to correspond with her about what they read. To make this approach work Henry not only has to build a classroom library, she has to immerse herself in the popular literature being read today in this country—science fiction, heaving-cleavage historical romance, gothic horror, blood and guts. She understands that in developing thoughtful readers "there are no shortcuts." Even if our goal is an appreciation of classical literature, the road there passes through (and regularly returns to) widely popular literature.

There are mistakes along the way that Henry candidly describes in a chapter called "Dirty Laundry." She shows us the tired, condescending, teacherly language that is easy to fall into. She shows how easy it is to dismiss a student's observation on our way to the point we want to make. One of the pleasures of this book is that she shows herself stumbling forward, falling on her face, then getting up with a smile and a joke.

We finish the book with a sense of admiration for her and her students. In a letter, one of them reflected on his high school years:

> I wish I could go back to my high school years and instead of sleeping and being silly I would have worked and gave 110%. But I can't, so I will have to deal with it. Yet it will haunt me a long time. There are no time machines.

True. But in this country, more than any other, students can have a second chance. In all of the national vilification of education, we sometimes forget the generosity of the system we choose to maintain. But if this second chance is to take, it cannot be a repetition of methods that at best produced aliteracy the first time around. We cannot act like tourists who think we can be understood if we repeat what we say, only louder.

There are no time machines. But Henry's course—these letters, this pleasure in reading—is the next best thing.

Thomas Newkirk
Durham, N.H.

Preface

Notes on Genesis

In some ways, this book is just a more reader-friendly version of the doctoral dissertation I completed in late 1992. Now, as then, I examine the literary letters exchanged between eighteen college reading students and me, their teacher, over the course of a semester-long reading improvement class that used Nancie Atwell's reading workshop approach, which she details in her book *In the Middle*. In rewriting my dissertation, I took a slash-and-burn approach to getting rid of its required academic elements. I want other teachers to meet my students and to learn from them, as I have, and I know teachers just do not have time to hack their way through a jungle of jargon before getting to the point. It was important for me to write all those missing pages we Pile Higher and Deeper in pursuit of advanced degrees, because they made me think through my design and my conclusions, but there is no need for anyone else to dig through them now. Another difference between this book and the dissertation is that I am now free to go beyond my "data." Although we have this idea that research is frozen in time, I did not stop learning just because my study ended, and the study itself taught me what to look for in the classes that followed. Here and there, I will tell you what my findings have come to mean over time.

The focus of this book, and of the study that put most of the meat on its bones, is the content of the four hundred and twenty literary letters these eighteen students and I exchanged. But even as I say that, I recognize that the study covered more terrain than just the letters and my findings revealed more about underprepared college students than I would have guessed. These students come to life in their letters, and their words reveal an achingly simple belief that college will bring them respect and prosperity. They worked too many hours, had little guidance in preparing themselves for college, and had made life choices that only made pursuing an education that much harder, but you will see that they are also people who know how to fix cars, raise children, work as volunteer firefighters, play in rock bands, and keep the American service industry running smoothly. Their inexperience as readers is sobering, but what these students have to say about how reading is taught in America, as well as their transformation from nonreaders into readers, will move you a little closer to the edge of your seat.

Notes on Structure

In Chapter 1, "The Road to Reading," I describe my experiences as a brand-new, know-nothing developmental reading teacher. I took the typical reading skills textbook I was handed and ran with it—straight into a brick wall. I wanted to believe I was helping students, but instead I was bewildered by just what these skills we drilled were supposed to be accomplishing. And as any other malcontent can tell you, it is easier to know what to reject than to know what to embrace. I talk about the trial of my errors and the journey that led me to Louise Rosenblatt's transactional theory and Nancie Atwell's *In the Middle*. Rosenblatt's theory that reading entails both public and private meanings, along with Atwell's reading workshop approach, with its free reading selection, individualized instruction, and literary letters, suddenly made theory and practice square for me. I discuss my decision to experiment with reading workshop in one of my college reading classes, as well as how I made the call to study workshop and literary letters for my dissertation research.

When I talk about Atwell's workshop at college reading conferences, what I hear over and over again is, "It sounds wonderful, but it would never work here." So, I thought it was important to study and to describe the particular classroom on the particular campus in the particular community in which these letters were written. I would be surprised to find that the view from here, Northern Kentucky University, is really so different from there. I think teachers everywhere will recognize my students, with their backwards ball caps, bomber jackets, sometimes single-digit ACT scores, and robust hostility toward the act of reading. This is what I discuss in Chapter 2, "The View from Here." Bottom line, the difference between my students and first graders, in terms of how to encourage them to read, amounts to little more than my students are bigger, sexually active, and pay bills. In terms of other adult learners, my students' peers in other words, it is the institutions that vary in profound ways, not the learners. I think we have to stay clear about that. Using the workshop approach might be controversial, treasonable, or even impossible at your school, but it would work. There is a big difference between "won't work here" and "can't happen here." We need to be on the same page about "won't" and "can't."

As the workshop unfolds in Chapter 3, "Reading Workshop," you will get a feel for the approach, its rhythms, and the rituals that serve as its structure. You will hear about my minilessons, everything from reading process to prediction, and you will be able to distinguish the ones I made up in the car from the ones that had the works, overheads and all. You will sit in on a "status of the class" check, in which I ask the students what they are reading that day, and you will see the students turn this check-in into something halfway between a reading competition and stand-up comedy. And you can sit beside me for those first few minutes of reading, when the students fidget, tear pages from their notebooks, and turn their backpacks inside out in search of some essential item until, finally, they settle into the most beautiful silence on earth, that of students engrossed in their reading. Although how we do things at NKU is not the end of the road, I talk about how we put together our class libraries, pay for books, and organize book-buying expeditions with our classes.

Chapter 4, "Buckets O' Blood," was my favorite to write. Here I talk about what the students in that first workshop class read and how I learned from them, along with later students, to predict undergraduate tastes so that my class library is filled with irresistible books. For example, I learned that hit movies make for popular workshop novels. Now, in October 1994, this means the hottest books in my class are *The Client*, *Natural Born Killers*, and *Forrest Gump*. In this chapter I also describe some of the purposes to which my students put their reading, everything from fixing cars to coming to grips with their sexual orientation to dealing with the death of a child. Tell students to read whatever matters to them, then be prepared when they do exactly that. I end Chapter 4 with my explanation of why these hard-core nonreaders suddenly started taking to this business of having their nose in a book. I have some unpleasant things to say about the kind of reading we ask students to do in school, and I speculate that academic reading, and how we teach it, may be what put them off books in the first place.

Chapter 5, "Literary Letters," is my favorite chapter to read because students do most of the talking. Here, I use excerpts from their letters to give an overview of what transpires in the literary-letter exchange. I learned that my students import features of real-world correspondence into their literary letters, such as indignation at unanswered mail. I talk about how interactive the letters are, since students are clearly writing to me, Jeanne Henry, not just some abstract "teacher," and I to them. This chapter then gets down to business by examining the content of students' letters, which I categorize as summary, interpretation, or observations about their own reading. Finally, I get to talk about what I think all this means, and my conclusion is that the field of reading has so focused on comprehension, which means to "take in" meaning, that we have failed to consider how our students "construct" meaning, especially when they are reading what they want to rather than what we assign. What we miss, in so doing, is discovering our students' strengths as readers. We are so busy trying to figure out and to correct what is "wrong" that we neglect to find out what is "right" when they read for their own purposes, for their own pleasure, and at their own pace.

Chapter 6 is called "Dirty Laundry," because here I hang mine on the line. One thing about doing teacher research is that you have to turn on the high beams and take a good look at your own work. And let me tell you, it plays hell with your "outstanding teacher" fantasies. I learned that in spite of my seeming theoretical certainty, I undermined my own beliefs about reading in the literary letters I exchanged with students in several different ways. Teacher training dies hard, like dandelions, and scrutiny is the only way to dig up the roots. I talk about how I corrected the mistakes I saw myself making, as well as a few things theory and research suggest I was doing right. I then describe how reading workshop nudged me out of the typical teacher roles of expert and evaluator and into the roles of collaborator, consultant, and witness.

Chapter 7, "Decision Time," examines the dilemma college and other reading teachers face. We are expected to teach students academic literacy, which more or less means reading textbooks, primary sources, and quite a few other things students are loath to read. In a quarter or a semester, we are supposed to take students from reading next to nothing to reading difficult, demanding, and sometimes personally irrelevant works. This is not possible, and you know it as well as I do. But what am I doing with reading workshop? Getting nonreaders to devour Danielle Steel and John Grisham. What has that got to do with academic reading? I have answered the question for myself, in that I do not think there are any shortcuts. Only practice and experience make students proficient and insightful readers. But neither teachers nor students have the luxury of the time this takes. For me, the decision is to do what I can do, which is to get nonreaders excited about reading. Maybe I cannot do my job, as it was prescribed, but wondrous things can happen for my students as readers if I keep the bigger picture—reading for the love rather than merely the utility of it—in view. And I do believe that my students can get from A to Z, aliteracy to academic literacy, but only in their own sweet time. I may not help students succeed in college, perhaps none of us really do, but I know that the weeks we spend reading together open my students' minds and eyes to having words come to life, to seeing stories unfold in their heads. I ignore unreal expectations and am satisfied. That is the essence of the decision I think we reading teachers have to make.

Notes on the Narrative

I had better explain a few things about anonymity and how it works in this book. Throughout, I use real names for colleagues unless I have something nasty to say about them, in which case I use no name at all. Given that I am writing about a real place (one I very thinly disguised for the dissertation), there really is no way to disguise the identities of the faculty I work with and, as long as I am saying something nice, no need to. With regard to students, however, I went to the extreme in terms of providing what one of them called "cloaking devices." At the end of the semester, when I asked my students for written consent to use their letters for research, they upped the ante by asking me to make sure that no one would recognize them, not even their classmates. I agreed and, to that end, I periodically switch the pseudonyms I use for students. A woman called "Kim" in one discussion might be "Valerie" in another. Someone who was in the class might remember that so-and-so read *Wealth Without Risk* and might then conclude "Kim" was that individual, but then so-and-so did not read *The Color Purple*, the next book I attribute to "Kim." I stayed true to gender, since I did not think I could credibly say that the writing of a female was that of a male or vice versa, but the five male and thirteen female pseudonyms I use in this book are interchangeable within their respective genders.

My efforts to avoid identifying my students will probably make readers furious, if it is true, as I suspect, that human nature practically demands that we "construct" the people we read about. You are going to think you know "Holly" or "Joanie" or "Mac" as early as Chapter 2. But this is not the case. You will "know" these eighteen students in fragments, rich glimpses into how developmental students at this institution, in this class, at this time, wrote about what they read, but you could not pick them out of a lineup, nor, I am confident, could they. This is the way they wanted it. My preference would have been to introduce each of them to the world, because they were smart and wonderful people, but I have respected their privacy, as they wished.

Chapter 1

The Road to Reading

In 1985, two days before classes were to start, I was hired to teach developmental reading at Northern Kentucky University. My previous experience had been teaching composition and creative writing, but I needed a better job than I had, and I figured that since I knew how to read well enough, I ought to be able to teach reading. Okay, that was naïveté knocking on arrogance's door, but I was to pay for it. I was shown to my new office, handed the college reading textbook my colleagues were using, as well as a course syllabus, and told where I could find the photocopying machine. I was all set. I had taught part-time at Northern the year before, so I was familiar with our working-class, commuter students, but developmental learners were new to me, and I immediately liked the way these students shot straight from the hip—asking me if I were old enough to be a college teacher (I was twenty-four) and telling me that reading "sucked." I thought I could swing with these students, creating the kind of irreverent, high-energy class I preferred.

My first inkling that something was going wrong with my teaching, however, was that I was bored (and sometimes floored) by it. Class discussions about paragraph organization left me numb, as did disputes about the main idea of a passage, which I usually had to settle by looking up the answer in the teacher's manual. What we did was dull, and what we called what we did was "reading." I wondered what I had gotten myself into. And, to be sure, there is nothing quite so clock-watching miserable for a teacher as the realization that what

1

she is doing in her classroom is useless. Nor did futility sit well with me, when I finally concluded that the skills-oriented approach I was using, while it did not seem to annoy my students, was not having the desired effect on their reading. They still hated to read, and I knew they were in no way ready for the parade of college textbooks that awaited them, no matter how much their Nelson-Denny (a commonly used placement/diagnostic test for college-level reading, vocabulary, and rate) scores improved. Sure, they could identify a main idea at five hundred paces, and they learned their vocabulary words, practicing them with the precision of a Texas drill team. But in spite of these new skills, my students often remained unable to make heads or tails of the passages we read.

At the end of that year, as I sat in my office reviewing my teaching evaluations, which were excellent, I felt like a criminal. My students would not read to save their lives, but a boost in their Nelson-Denny scores had convinced them I was a great teacher and that mine was a great class. I knew better. And I was not the first to think so. College reading textbooks published and widely used within the United States give you the impression that teaching reading subskills, like main idea identification, paragraph organization, and random vocabulary acquisition, is the ticket. But in a 1988 meta-analysis, Stahl, Simpson, and Brozo (1988, 31) came to several conclusions about college reading instruction as it is presented in textbooks. First, the theoretical model of reading underlying all this to-do about reading subskills in most textbooks is not alluded to and impossible to infer. Second, there is not much in the way of research evidence to recommend most of the techniques advocated in these books. Third, the transfer value of the practice activities provided in these texts is questionable. These colleagues conclude that college reading is a "curriculum of tradition as opposed to a curriculum driven by current applied research and/or theory."

So is it any wonder that after I read through my evaluations that day, I took all the college reading textbooks off the bookshelves in my office and dropped them one at a time into the trash can with a "bomb's away" whistle. My program director stopped by and said, "Are you reforming the curriculum or having a nervous breakdown?" "A bit of both," I answered, and went about my business. The day I threw away those reading books, what I now call "basals for big people," marked my absolute rejection of the prevailing skills-oriented approach to teaching college reading. But it is a long way from there to here, and the steps that led to my eventual and timely (from a mental health perspective) adoption of Nancie Atwell's reading workshop convey the urgency with which I conducted the teacher research that makes up most of the rest of this book.

Knowing what approach to reject was one thing, but replacing it with something better was beyond what I knew how to do. About all I was certain of in 1985 was that what I called reading when there was a book in front of my nose was very different from the kind of reading I taught in my classroom. What I wanted for my students was to broaden their image of "reader" from that of some dead-from-the-neck-down stiff to include my neighbor Deedy, who kept a battered copy of *Walden* strapped to her muddy mountain bike. I thought their sense of "reader" ought to include English majors like Michelle Robinson, who alternated books by Virginia Woolf and Toni Morrison with books that had pirates and lots of cleavage on the cover. And it was my will that my students see Aunt Doris, whose boredom with failing health and old age was relieved by novels of love and intrigue. I wanted them to see that millions of other readers, just like them, were curious about murderous minds, recovering from failed relationships, and conflicted about sex before marriage. I wanted them to see themselves—parents, hourly wage workers, sports enthusiasts, and mall cruisers—as people who also loved to read. But how was I to teach what they could only experience?

Not knowing what else to do, I experimented in the classroom, listened to my colleagues voice their concerns about the skills approach, and learned as much as I could. I read Frank

Smith, the Goodmans, and Louise Rosenblatt (more about that later), and I enrolled in a doctoral program in literacy at the University of Cincinnati. All of these efforts provided me with theoretical support for my intuitive rejection of the skills approach, but it was really students, and what I learned from working with them, that contributed heat, light, and energy to my growing sense of what reading was and how to teach it. First there was DeWayne, a second grader whose teacher had assessed him as a low- to nonreader. DeWayne and I came together in a graduate practicum taught by Victoria Purcell-Gates. The purpose of this three-quarter course was to teach assessment techniques and strategies for reading improvement in the context of working with real students. Vickie's brilliant and invaluable touch—in spite of the case of chicken pox De-Wayne gave me—was to insist that we work with students who were outside our previous teaching experience. Vickie wanted us to have a sense of reading instruction from the sandbox to that black rayon gown, so that we would know where our students were headed and whence they had come.

During one of our very first sessions, DeWayne and I were kicked back, contemplating a gray winter day, when I suggested he read me "A Snowy Day," since we both liked winter best when there was snow. DeWayne had not read aloud to me before, and I needed to weigh his teacher's assessment of his reading. The kid slaughtered the story, mistaking *that* for *the*, *shoe* for *snow*, and *cat* for *coat*. I went ahead with the rest of the protocol and asked DeWayne to retell the story. What I heard left me shaking my head in disbelief. His retelling was flawless. He could not read the words to save his life, but he understood them. The words, the parts, were incidental to the whole, the meaning. DeWayne's skills-oriented teacher had assumed—as her training told her she should—that his inability to manage the parts meant understanding the whole was out of the question. What most distressed me was that DeWayne also believed he could not read much, if at all. *His* understanding of reading was getting distorted by what he was being taught. You will be relieved to know that by the end of our year together, DeWayne's teacher concluded he was reading at "grade level"; but what had changed was his ability to read words aloud, not his teacher's understanding of reading, which was that reading skills were sequential, entirely driven by the sound/symbol relationship, and the product of direct instruction.

Another hammer-to-the-head insight about the problems with the part-to-whole thinking of skills instruction was delivered by my college students. I have gotten a lot of mileage out of the following sentence: "Mariemont, a suburb of Cincinnati, is one of those theme communities in which even the Catholic Church has given up its grudge and gone Tudor" (Henry 1990, 425), and I now use it in a minilesson to demonstrate to students that being able to read the words is no guarantee that their meaning will be understood. The words of the Mariemont sentence are simple, readily definable, and easily pronounceable, but the problem is that their cumulative meaning resides in a knowledge of the Protestant Reformation in England, not in the words. My students can read these words all day long, highlight, summarize, or paraphrase them, but they still will not know what the sentence is getting at. Decades of reading instruction fizzled as fast as a firecracker in the snow once I acknowledged that reading words and making meaning were not one and the same.

Really, what I was learning was that there were no shortcuts. The skills approach, invented sometime before women got the vote, was an effort to substitute direct instruction for direct experience in a sincere effort to help those who were "behind" catch up quickly. But there is no substitute for experience. I can teach you to ski by having you practice isolated skills, such as jump turns, on a bunny slope, but if that is the only experience you have before I rush you up to an expert-only run, I might as well just kill you outright. It is a little like teaching students to identify paragraph organization in a short reading passage one semester and then sending them off to a sociology class the next and expecting them to read and fully understand Christopher Lasch's *Culture of Narcissism*.

And then there is the affective angle. Imagine that you have skied a few times but found those initial lessons—the snow-plow, the snow-eat, and the snow-get-up—uninteresting, humiliating, and frustrating—as most adults do. You feel idiotic at the lodge, carrying around your short little beginner skis, when everyone else is complaining that the runs are too easy at this particular resort. Why, it's a little like asking a college student to walk around campus carrying a book called *Improving Your Reading Skills*. So, to persuade you to give skiing another try, I could describe the view from atop Mt. Cook in New Zealand, where it feels as if you are at the very top of the very bottom of the world. Or maybe I could describe how gravity and velocity make for an electrifying descent. But I cannot *give* you the physical or mental experience, in order to make you crave more of the same, any more than I could hand over my pleasure in reading to my students.

I became convinced that the only way my students could improve their reading was if they read. And even though they dutifully read whatever I asked them to, they were doing "homework," not reading. I assigned a lot of material, as much as I thought the traffic would bear, but my students needed to read for themselves, not for me, and reading had to become a habit, something they could not leave alone. So, my next questions were, Why do those of us who enjoy reading savor it as we do? What was missing for my students? I began shopping around for a theory of reading that would help me understand those parts of reading not found in the skills approach or in the data-driven and interactive models of reading loosely associated with it. A shopping list of what I was looking for would have read something like this: I wanted a theory of reading that explained why my friend Susan Sieney read Anne Rice's *Interview with the Vampire* and was so mesmerized by the world Rice created that she had fantasies of becoming a vampire. (Okay, so did I, but it was even weirder with Susan, since she is vegetarian.) I wanted a theory of reading that could account for why books like *Even Cowgirls Get the Blues, Radical Chic, Tales of the City*, and *Fear and Loathing in Las Vegas* had been so irresistible when I was in college that my friends and I read them in a single day. What were we looking for? What were we finding? And why had these books lit such a fire under us to find others like them? I wanted a theory that explained reading the way modern physics explains reality, as inseparable from the human mind observing it. Think about this. It takes the light from the sun about eight minutes and twenty seconds to travel the ninety million miles to earth, but to the observer, there is no delay: sunlight is *happening*, not history. When we read, all we are looking at, in a concrete sense, are symbols on a page, but books *happen* to us. Michelle, my student assistant, finds herself in the arms of a pirate as she reads, and I feel werewolves nipping at my heels whenever I am not socially adept enough to avoid politely the horror books my students recommend to me. I know people who read history, geography, and anthropology with as much imaginative recklessness as Michelle reads fiction. Where was the theory of reading that explained the alchemy of turning symbol into sensation?

I ended up finding more satisfying answers about the reading process in literary rather than reading theory, and my theoretical "home" turned out to be Louise Rosenblatt's transactional theory. In 1987, Karin Dahl, one of my doctoral committee members, handed me Rosenblatt's *Literature as Experience* (1968) and said, "Read this book. I think it's what you've been looking for." And it was. Here was a theory that described reading as a collaboration between reader and text. Marilyn Sternglass explained it best when she wrote that readers are "creating new meanings as they interact with texts, meanings that did not exist independently before either in the mind of the author or the reader" (1986, 151). Let me use this chapter as an example. You are reading about my teaching experiences here, but what you may be paying more attention to as you read are your own frustrations with or aspirations for your teaching. Or you may be locked in mortal mental combat with me, deploying your proskills arguments and wielding your highlighter like a weapon, dousing every dumb thing I have to say with yellow ink. Maybe you are thinking about a student of yours or the last book you read. Your reveries, whether they are digressions, connections, associations, or counterarguments, are all a part of the meanings you make, meanings Rosenblatt would call private because they are too individual to be shared by (although they can be shared with) other readers. Your meanings certainly were not in my head as I wrote this, and perhaps these thoughts had never come together for you in precisely the same way before this text set off the chain of events that it did, but the meaning we produced, together, is the new event Sternglass is talking about. You will not find your meanings on a comprehension test, because they are too individual, which renders them inconvenient when it comes to the mass-produced, multiple-choice meanings we have chosen to focus all our attention on in reading instruction. But your meanings are as real as sunlight.

Transactional theory explains the way we arrive at these private meanings, as well as how we come up with what Rosenblatt calls public, or shared, meanings. Rosenblatt describes a "linguistic-experiential reservoir" from which readers select both the public and private meanings they associate with the words found on a page. The public meaning of a word is the "tip of the iceberg," the literal, dictionary-type definition. Deep below, at the base of that iceberg, reside the private meanings of a word, those meanings that are formed by the personal, social, and cultural contexts in which we find ourselves (1989, 159). Think about the word *girl*. In a public sense, *girl* means a female child, but way below, in those layers of ice, reside many meanings for the word. When one of my male students here in Kentucky refers to his *girl*, what he means is his sweetheart. But when an executive across the river in Cincinnati talks about his *girl,* he means a secretary, not his beloved. In Atlanta, where I pondered both my adolescence and social justice, a *girl* was an African-American servant, regardless of her age. To feminists, like me, *girl* is a politically charged word sometimes mistakenly applied to adult women, and to the youngsters in the women's studies classes I also teach, *girl* is spelled and pronounced *grrrl,* in order to get in a growl of protest while at the same time reforming a demeaning label.

Depending on our reasons for reading, we may ignore our more personal meanings in favor of the public meaning of a word or words, or we may select those private meanings and run with them. If we did not have this ability to pay selective attention, we would be forever spinning off into word-by-word digressions. Rosenblatt's concept of stance is also helpful in understanding how we allocate our attention and why. The stance readers assume while reading flows along a continuum between "efferent" and "aesthetic." The reader's focus in primarily efferent reading is on what is to be "taken away" from the text, such as facts or concrete information. In primarily aesthetic reading, the reader's attention is focused on what is being "lived through *during* reading," whatever the text *evokes* in the mind and the heart of the reader (1985a, 70).

Let me try to illustrate stance with one of my favorite books. Don DeLillo's *Libra* is a fictional account of the mind, character, and actions of Lee Harvey Oswald. While reading this book, those who can remember the Kennedy assassination might read aesthetically, conjuring their memories of the event. "Where were you when Kennedy was killed?" In my crib, but other people have vivid memories of seeing a teacher, a parent, or Walter Cronkite cry after hearing the news. DeLillo's book convinced me that Oswald was a conspirator only in his own mind. A student who read the book when I did was born in 1970. He read *Libra* efferently, confronting me with the daily refrain: "Did you know . . ." that Oswald had lived in the Soviet Union, was in the Marine

Corps, had a Russian wife, and was killed shortly after the assassination by a man named Jack Ruby? For him, the book was a fact-finding mission that led him to read a half-dozen nonfiction accounts of the Kennedy years. My reading experience, along with that of my student, is different from that of a Dallas citizen who stood in the crowd admiring the First Lady's pink dress as the motorcade passed by that November day. Which of us understood the book better? Which interpretation was correct? Who enjoyed the book more or had a better reading experience?

Public meanings are essential in a complex world that has to communicate intelligibly, and efferent reading is very useful whenever we are being tested on what we have read or when we want to draw up a contract or learn to fix something. But the private meanings of words, and the deeply evocative readings they produce, are powerfully alluring, whether we are reading fiction or fact. They make reading happen, like sunlight and pirates. They keep reading from being like listening to a monologue, which most of us are willing to do only when we are deeply and newly in love. My hunch was that my students had had little opportunity to experience reading as a dialogue, the new event transactional theory described. Maybe this was because they did not read very well or were inexperienced, or maybe it was because they had never had the intellectual privacy to read without a teacher, preacher, or parent looking over their shoulders. Maybe they had been asked to read books that were too difficult or too distant from their own experience. But the pressing question was, How could I provide my students with the freedom and the flexibility to explore these other dimensions of reading? It seems absurd to me now, but I never once considered simply asking them to read—whatever they wanted, at their own pace, in class and out. I was still wed to the idea that I was the expert who had to lead the way, make the assignments, and find that book so irresistible twenty students would shed lifelong aliteracy.

Then in early 1988 I read Nancie Atwell's *In the Middle* (1987). Here was an approach to reading instruction that put to work my view that students needed the opportunity to read for their own purposes and to develop their own preferences. Atwell spoke like a reader, and what she wanted to share with her students was reading, not a curriculum. And what absolutely killed me was her mechanism for getting students to read: let them read, whatever they liked, without interference or interruption. It never would have occurred to me, as indoctrinated as I had been, to use reading class for reading rather than talking about reading. And, I saw, it was not up to me to find the books that would open the kingdom for my students—that was their job. Workshop created a reading environment rather than told me what to teach, and this was precisely the kind of opportunity my students needed: fifteen weeks to discover what pleasures, if any, reading might hold for them when they were reading the right books for the right reasons. The workshop atmosphere reminded me of the bookshelf in my childhood home, crammed with children's books and placed in the hallway between my brother's bedroom and mine, so that books would always be within easy reach. I remember sitting in that heavily trafficked hallway, reading for hours and talking about these books with whatever family member or friend happened by. This was where I had learned to love reading, and I saw that my classroom could be the same kind of place.

And light years ahead of my own thinking was Atwell's idea of literary letters. I had grown weary of the writing-about-reading activities generally used in skills approaches, which were limited to fill-in-the-blank responses intended to lead students in a particular interpretive direction or short essay answers with much the same purpose. And while I had switched to response journals in the course of my experimenting, I was aware of a new set of problems and limitations journals entailed. First, my students never seemed sure of their audience. Were they writing to me or some general readership? Second, were these journal entries intended to help them clarify their own thinking about an assignment, or were they supposed to be showing me that they had understood a passage in a particular way? I was never sure either, and my responses indicated irresolute acceptance of whatever a student had to say. And what was the point of asking a question in the margins, since these entries were "done" and we had moved on to the next set of readings and responses? What was the point of raising my own interpretive point of view, since I could never be sure my comments were read or understood? But these literary letters seemed like they might at least solve this issue of audience and, if I could reproduce Atwell's experience, they would entail actual dialogues between my students and me about what we were reading. Imagine talking about books with students in the same way I talked to my friends about what we were reading. I liked everything about workshop, but it was literary letters that most appealed to me. It seemed that whatever I had to offer as an experienced reader and as an advocate for these students might be communicated in these letters.

In general, I am much better at seizing opportunities when I recognize them than engaging in long-range planning, and so although I wanted to pilot reading workshop immediately, I waited a year. First, even though my colleagues would never interfere with what I did in my classroom, I wanted them to be a party to my experiment with workshop. I needed that year to share Atwell's ideas with them and to ask for their help in planning the pilot—everything from transforming reading workshop into something that could be explained in a college syllabus to how I could get books for a classroom library. I needed their wisdom and their help, but I also wanted them to be stakeholders in the experiment. And finally, as a doctoral student in search of a dissertation topic, I knew I wanted to take a good long look at the literary letters my students and I would eventually exchange, and I needed time to design the study and prepare a proposal. I also had to finesse my doctoral committee a little (very little—

they were as eager to learn about literary letters as I was), since I was proposing my dissertation research before I had even taken my qualifying exams. I toiled away that year, preparing a literature review, collecting books for my students, developing minilessons, and throwing away one syllabus after another, but by the 1989–90 academic year, I knew I was as ready for reading workshop as I was going to be. I took a deep breath and took the plunge.

❧ *Chapter 2*

The View from Here

Northern Kentucky University

Northern Kentucky University is a starkly modern campus of three hundred acres surrounded by one parking lot after another, a tip-off that this is a commuter campus. Beyond parking lots W, X, Y, and Z, farmland is rapidly being developed into middle-income apartment complexes and upper-income subdivisions. We have a commanding view atop the steep hill on which the university rests: the Cincinnati skyline is seven miles to the northwest and the rolling, blue-gray hills of Kentucky lie to the south. The buildings on campus are constructed of poured concrete, with jutting facades, little color, few windows, and sharp technocratic angles. They form a futuristic and formidable circle of stone. The first time I saw the campus, it put me in mind of a maximum security prison. I later learned that a folk legend circulated among students that the buildings were built to double as a prison, should the university fail. I was perpetually lost my first year at Northern, since I could not tell one building from another. If I asked which building was Natural Science, my colleagues would crack themselves up by saying, "The gray one." Ha ha. All the buildings are gray. Recent construction, though, has challenged the technical bravura of the architecture by disturbing land used for generations to graze livestock, allowing the bracing fragrance of manure to slice through the chilly winter air. Northern is the perfect fusion of the rural past and the increasingly urban future its students face. And like its students, the university is struggling with both insularity and image.

Established in 1968, Northern Kentucky University is situated three miles southeast of Covington and Newport and is the newest of Kentucky's eight universities. It has an open admissions policy—for the time being—which means that any high school graduate in the state is eligible to attend, regardless of grades, standardized test scores, or high school program followed. About twelve thousand students attend Northern, and within the walls of any building on Northern's grounds, you sense competing needs for space. In *Mao II*, Don DeLillo writes that "the future belongs to crowds," which may explain why Northern feels like such a vibrant campus. Twelve thousand students, while a small number in comparison with the population of most states' flagship universities, are a mob when their learning, studying, eating, record keeping, teaching, politicking, and socializing have to be conducted within a total of nine buildings. The campus is one of sound and fury, signifying uncertain economic times in the community and the promise of relief higher education holds out.

If you live in the The Greater Cincinnati–Northern Kentucky Area and you want to go to college, your most frugal choice is Northern, if you can stand the slings and arrows of such appellations as "No Knowledge College" or "Bedrock." The institution is in Kentucky, after all, and the mountain heritage of so many Kentuckians is regarded as incestuous or sociopathic by our how-*did*-they-get-so-sophisticated neighbors across the river in Ohio. Semester fees at Northern, entitling students up to eighteen credit hours, are just under nine hundred dollars. Northern's president, Leon Boothe, a dignified and avuncular figure on campus, has said that low tuition is, in effect, a way to give every student a scholarship. A recipient of Northern's outstanding professor award, Tom Zaniello, calls the university a "successful model of mass education." Northern serves a population that would not have considered going to college twenty years ago. Many of our students are the first in their families to attend college. Others are the first among their relations to have completed high school. Nearly a third of Northern students come from families earning less than thirty thousand dollars annually. And unlike the college experience of students in days gone by, over half of Northern's freshman class expects to work eleven to forty hours a week while attending school.

Right around forty percent of Northern students are over age twenty-five and juggle job and family responsibilities in addition to their schooling. When I first started teaching here, at age twenty-three, I was rattled about the fact that over a third of my students would be older than I was. I was sure they would realize how inexperienced I was. Maybe they did, but they also respected my education in a way that I had been much too privileged to do. Many of these "nontraditional" students had either been laid off from or injured at local industries like General Electric or Newport Steel. As a student who had been injured at the steel factory told me, "I thought I'd always earn my living with my back, but I've got to develop other skills now, at age forty-three. I've got news for these young guys dying to quit school and get on at UPS loading trucks for eighteen dollars an hour. It's no good for the long haul." Many other nontraditional students are single women with children. Laverne, a part-time student and custodial worker at Northern, summed up her aspirations: "I always thought I could do more than I am right now. And hopefully, when my kids see me studying and writing my papers, they'll know I mean it when I tell them an education is important, because they'll see me doing it."

A number of Northern students are of Appalachian descent, although many seem oblivious to their mountain heritage, which may be because of the anti-Appalachian stereotyping in the area. My students frequently accuse everybody else of being "hillbillies," despite the dead-giveaway trait of their own Appalachian heritage: fiercely intelligent eyes, of such a pure pale blue that it is a day's work just to look into them. Adrena Belcher, an Appalachian activist I talked to during the course of my research, told me that urban Appalachians cannot thrive wherever they are until they are permitted to take pride in where they are from. How long can any group of people be accused of a thirst for blood and a predilection toward incest without internalizing some of that loathing? There is no copy of *Deliverance* in my class library. Instead, I have multiple copies of the works of Jesse Stuart and Harriet Arnow's *The Dollmaker*. Fewer than one percent of Northern students and faculty are African American. As Desmond, an African American sophomore put it, "I kept thinking there had to be some sort of CP hangout I didn't know about. Then I figured it out. The *other* black guy in your class, well, him and you, that's it."

Ted Weiss, a recently promoted full professor in geography, known for his genuine love of teaching and high regard for students, says that Northern undergraduates "say appalling things about groups of people but are uncommonly accepting of one another's differences on a one-to-one basis." My students sharpened Ted's point less than two weeks after he made it. A fire alarm sounded during class one day, and my instructions for evacuating students were to leave those who were wheelchair-bound in the stairwell for later evacuation. While none of my students believed there was a fire, all were outraged that they were supposed to leave their immobile classmates behind. I intervened as a group of ten students prepared to hoist our two wheelchair-bound classmates, determined to carry them down a flight of stairs. Naturally the students in the wheelchairs thought this was a kick and were all for playing hot potato down the stairs; but while I admired the other students' concern, I had visions of emergency medical technicians dancing in my head. I persuaded them that since there really was no fire, we could just wait together on the stairs until campus security cleared a return to our classroom. These young people were from the same student body that complained, in letters to the editor in the student newspaper, that electronic doors for the disabled, which stayed open for sixty seconds, let too much cold air into the cafeteria and should be dismantled.

Academically, Northern students have respectable credentials but are consistently below national means on the ACT. As an open admissions institution, Northern enrolls a number of "underprepared" students. And this university, like any center of higher learning, has some gifted undergraduates. A former women's studies student of mine is now in Indonesia conducting research, and another was recently accepted into George Mason's graduate program in poetry writing. One of my former developmental reading students just completed his master's degree in urban planning at Ohio State University. Yet another reading student of mine, a graduating senior who was president of student government last year and student regent this year, will probably be the governor of Kentucky one day, in which case I hope he will stop a recent gubernatorial trend to punish, exclude, surcharge, discourage, or further marginalize those students who did not manage to excel in an impoverished and inadequate state educational system.

My sense is that many of Northern's students are not seeking the abstraction of "an education" that my parents generously handed me. There was never any doubt that I would go to college. In fact, I was never asked if I wanted to go. The only question was *where* I *would* go. For many of Northern's students, though, college is a wait-and-see issue. Do they have the grades to justify the expense and/or to delay their full-time earning potential? Do they have career aspirations that require a college education? Will a college education really help them improve the quality of their lives? And, for a few, the question is, What else can they do right now but go to school? since they need to mature a bit before moving out of the family home and obtaining a job they cannot afford to lose. Most of our students associate respect and achievement with earning a college degree, but they go to college because their dreams are of financial security, owning some nice things, and doing interesting work that makes use of their talents.

NKU's Learning Assistance Program

Northern's Learning Assistance Program offers developmental reading and writing courses, along with peer tutoring in writing, study skills, and academic subjects. The program is not very visible on campus, and I sometimes wonder if our colleagues even know the university offers developmental reading courses. I think the benign neglect the program experiences (until we do outrageous things like ask for tenure) is typical of that experienced by many other developmental programs. Programs for the underprepared, no matter how innovative or exceptional, just are not the ones a university wants to showcase. To get hung up about it (even if one senior administrator consistently mistakes you for a psychology professor who is ten pounds heavier and at least ten years older) is to need to find yourself another line of work. Developmental faculty should always lobby for better pay and more recognition, given that our salaries seem to be determined by some weird correlation with our students' ACT scores, but to take a lack of professional recognition personally will erode your life and your work. Morale in Learning Assistance is high because *we* think we are swell. The two directors I have worked under, Fran Zaniello and Paul Ellis, have kept us out of pedagogical ruts by never letting us take the easy way out, a course easily justified by low pay and too little attention. Both Fran and Paul have pushed for reflective practice and constant improvement.

Learning Assistance was and still is a small program, with only six full-time faculty (one director, three writing instructors, and two reading instructors), about a half-dozen veteran adjuncts, and Mrs. Holtz, program secretary. Two of the full-time faculty, one of them me, have been reassigned to administrative positions, which has been a hardship for Learning Assistance, even though I still teach three reading courses each year. Things have changed so much in the program since I piloted and studied reading workshop that it is tough to decide whether I should talk about then or now. I suppose

I should say a little about both. Just before I piloted the reading workshop, only three of us taught reading, either full- or part-time. One instructor used a traditional skills-oriented method, and the other took sort of a New Criticism approach to textual analysis. Meanwhile, I was busy campaigning for a shot at using the workshop approach. Back then, the reading course was called LAP 091: Reading Improvement. Now the course is called LAP 091: Reading Workshop. Then and now, students are required to take LAP 091 based on their ACT scores. All developmental courses carry institutional rather than academic credit (in other words, they do not count toward graduation), but students do receive letter grades. Grades for developmental courses are not figured into a student's graduating GPA, nor are they considered when calculating honors. But in a slick double standard, the grades *are* factored into the student's GPA when it comes to making decisions about academic probation and/or suspension.

Just before I piloted reading workshop, then-director of Learning Assistance, Fran Zaniello, asked me to profile our developmental reading students. We knew our students despised reading, but she wanted a means of documenting the hunches that had us both sizing up workshop as a means of breaking through our students' resistance. So, fresh out of my doctoral research design and statistics classes, I developed a survey about students' reading attitudes and practices. We administered the survey to the one hundred seventy-six students enrolled in developmental reading that following semester. What we learned was that right around half of the students reported that they "never" read for pleasure. Roughly a third of our students were from homes that did not encourage reading, and another third of the students liked people who read about as much as they liked debt-collection agencies; in other words, thirty-one percent of these college freshmen agreed with the statement, "I feel hostility toward people who read a lot."

Now that last one got to us. Resistance theory probably applies here. These students had seen a "member's only" sign somewhere and were feeling kind of cranky about it. Maybe that sign was the sense that they could not be readers if they disliked what a teacher had deemed worthy literature. Possibly they heard what they did like to read belittled as "trash." Or maybe it was that they never got all the answers right, since right answers have come to mean so much in reading and literature classes. Perhaps they felt excluded from or indifferent to the stories they were asked to read—stories about a world peopled exclusively by whites, males, heterosexuals, the middle class. For some, it may have felt more clean to reject those who devalued them than to assimilate dishonestly, regardless of the consequences. An avid reader from way back, I had resisted my relentlessly irrelevant high school English classes rather than reading itself, but I could still understand. And so could Fran. After examining the survey, we could not get workshop going fast enough.

The Uneasy Here and Now

When I talk about reading workshop at conferences and about how Learning Assistance has now institutionalized the approach (as well as an Atwell-inspired writing workshop and an integrated reading/writing workshop for students required to take both developmental classes), other teachers think I work in a pedagogical paradise. But paradise gets a bit tense at times. Even though the catalogue description of our reading course now describes an Atwell-inspired workshop, my two longtime reading colleagues still use the approaches I ascribed to them a few paragraphs ago. They consider the workshop irresponsible. It is writing faculty, retrained to teach integrated reading/writing courses, along with new hires, who offer sections of Reading Workshop that actually operate as workshops. A student enrolling in LAP 091: Reading Workshop might get a class in which she reads whatever she chooses and exchanges literary letters with the teacher or a class in which she underlines main ideas and takes vocabulary quizzes or a class in which she participates in line-by-line textual analysis led by the teacher. The unspoken agreement seems to be that forcing another teacher to follow an approach that she clearly rejects would destroy both her pleasure in teaching and her effectiveness. But a lot goes unsaid these days. A faculty that used to talk about teaching all the time must now recognize that to so do is to risk upsetting a delicate balance. I mention this only because I know that whole language practitioners—the school of thought to which I attribute workshop—and skills teachers are squaring off all over the country, at every grade level. All of us are sincere, but we suspect that the other camp is sincerely *wrong*. Conflict is very apparent in journals and at conferences, but the face-to-face, career- and friendship-ending confrontations still await. No one is looking forward to these times.

❧ *Chapter 3*

Reading Workshop

The first day of reading workshop did not start like any other day. I woke up feeling tense and tired, after a night of second thoughts about the theory I trusted but had not tested. I was uncertain about how to explain workshop procedures to students, as well as how they would react to a course unlike any other they had taken. As I went through my morning routines, I rehearsed how I would justify the course procedures by explaining that the only means of improving reading was willing practice. "I want you to give reading another chance," I said as I plugged in the coffeepot and prepared to give my ancient dog her daily injection of Lasix. The dog, taking advantage of my preoccupation, did that crawl-on-her-belly-like-a-snake thing dogs do and avoided the syringe, which instead slammed home into my own leg. At least I quit worrying about workshop, since I suddenly had a couple of other priorities, like yelling at a deaf dog to come back, phoning the vet to see what effect Lasix might have on me, and preparing another syringe. Lasix is a diuretic. Never in my career had I so wanted to dismiss a class early as I did on that first day of workshop.

Less than an hour later, I burst into my classroom. "Hey, is this LAP 091, Reading Improvement?"

A few students nodded.

"And this is room 333, and it's nine o'clock on Monday, and your schedules say your teacher is named Henry?"

A few more nods.

I moved to the front of the room. "I've got the syllabus and we're all in the right room. Doesn't get much better than this." When I finally looked around the room, I realized the students had that stunned look a former vice-president made famous a few years ago with his wide, unblinking eyes. I asked a few innocuous questions, like if parking had been much of a problem, and they paused for a full fifteen seconds before answering, as if they suspected a trap. So I simply launched into my speech about how this was an experimental course, and then I went over the features of reading workshop. I told the students they could read whatever they wanted, as long as they read, and that most of our class time would be devoted to reading. I explained that I would start each class with a minilesson about reading and that we would write letters to each other about our books.

I asked if there were any questions. There should have been about a hundred. That was when their silence began to seem sinister. I scanned the silent room, looking for signs of life and thinking, Where have you hidden your pods? But I smiled as if I suspected nothing and went on to explain how the students would set goals for themselves and then have an opportunity to evaluate their own performance. I again asked if there were any questions. Nothing. I was just about to capitulate and agree to be taken to their leader when a rubber band I had been stretching between my fingers suddenly flew out of my hands and, to my horror, hit a young man on the shoulder. He stared at me for a moment, then said, "Uh . . . do I get extra credit for that?" Vital signs returned. Nothing like the teacher's acting a total fool to loosen up a class. When I asked again if there were any questions, Valerie raised her hand.

"Let me get this straight," she said in a voice that suggested too little sleep, too many cigarettes, and more trouble in the last ten days than I had seen in the last ten years. "We can read anything we want to, as long as we read?"

I nodded. "What's your name?"

"Valerie."

"You look skeptical, Valerie."

"Well, I was in this other reading class yesterday, but I dropped it because this was a better time. And this other teacher is making them read from a book about how to read better. And they have to take vocabulary quizzes and comprehension tests," she said.

"You think I'm gonna pull a fast one?"

Valerie smiled and shrugged. "First thing that come to mind when you said we could read anything was Stephen King. Everybody says he's good. So I can read one of his books?"

"Sure," I said. "I've never read any Stephen King, but I will if you will."

We spent the rest of the class skimming the course syllabus, a four-page document I was completely out of my mind for thinking any of them would ever read. But the students had a chance to get a good look at me, and I at them. Of the twenty-one students who showed up that first day, eighteen eventually made it through the course and became part of the study: five men, including Ray, a student who had failed my course the previous semester, and thirteen women. Valerie and two other women over age thirty sat in the front of the room; the rest of the women, ranging from eighteen to twenty-four years, were scattered about. Three of the eighteen students were African American, one was Korean, and the other fourteen were mostly second- and third-generation urban Appalachians—a categorization they dispensed with but did not dispute.

As is true for all my classes, Student Support Services, a federally funded campus agency that provides counseling and academic assistance to students who are physically handicapped, learning disabled, poor, or first-generation college enrollees, had placed a number of their students in my charge. Stephanie Baker, who directed the program at the time, told me she put her students in my classes because

"Nothing phases you. You think random capitalization is sign of a creative mind." Two students in the class were wheelchair-bound, and three were single, teenaged parents. A couple of the students were recovering from drug or alcohol addictions, and eight more had been identified as having learning disabilities ranging from so-called attention deficit disorder to so-called dyslexia. One student, who had recently sustained a severe closed skull brain injury, had profound memory problems, and another was suffering from clinical depression. Dave openly referred to the class as the "trauma ward," which pretty much says it all in terms of the students' candor about their difficulties.

The class met three days a week, from 9:00 to 9:50 A.M., and although I had done most of the talking the first day and was eager to get students reading, I had to administer the Nelson-Denny, since all Northern's developmental reading classes were then pre- and posttested with this legendary instrument. We never made much use of the data we collected with the Nelson-Denny. None of us saw it as the oracle others in the profession seemed to, but one of my responsibilities was to collect each teacher's Nelson-Denny results at the end of the semester and compile the descriptive statistics. No administrator ever asked to see the results, and no instructor was ever asked to account for her students' performance, but testing is something you do in reading classes, and so we tested away.

I sat watching as my students took the Nelson-Denny during the second day of class. I presented the test seriously and objectively. But as I read along with my students, discretely watching them, I saw and heard Kelly mutter "Dude's a freak" in response to the passage about Percy Byshe Shelley. After collecting the Nelson-Denny responses, I passed out an informal reading attitude inventory developed by Nancie Atwell (1987, 271–72), and asked students to return it the next class. I had added a few more questions to Atwell's inventory, such as whether or not students used their county libraries. As I scored my students' Nelson-Dennys, I was relieved to discover that my students were average in every way, as common as sinus infections in the Midwest. Banality is very helpful for research purposes, because it means you have less to account for. My program normed raw scores against the Grade 13, Four-Year University population. On reading comprehension, the entering average for my class, in grade-level equivalents, was 8.6. This was in keeping with the entering average of Northern's reading students throughout the four years I had been keeping statistics. And to get this out of the way, allow me to jump ahead fifteen weeks to the posttest. My students' exiting average on reading comprehension was 12.2 (in grade-level equivalents), which indicated a "gain" of 3.6 grade levels in fifteen weeks of reading workshop.

As I read through the responses to the reading attitude inventory, it was clear that my students were about as willing to read as college administrators are to fund developmental programs. Most of them hated to read and never read for pleasure; only three had read an entire book in the previous year. One of the questions I added to Atwell's inventory was if the student had a library card. The question was meant to be pragmatic. Since I did not yet have a vast stockpile of books for my class library, I realized students would need to borrow books elsewhere and I wanted to identify those who needed library cards. What I learned instead was that *none* of my students had a card. I immediately told students that they could earn extra credit by acquiring a library card and could double the credit by using the card. Now I do a minilesson every semester on the location of county libraries and the procedures for obtaining borrowing privileges. If time permits, I take my workshop classes across the river on a field trip to Cincinnati to obtain cards at that city's truly outstanding main library, only seven miles from campus.

Another question I added to Atwell's inventory was whether or not the students had been read to as children.

Only three had. And of the five mothers in the class, none read to her child. My response, as this "finding" has been pretty consistent with every class since, is to read aloud to my students once in a while. We sit together on the floor, and I usually read stories by Kentucky authors, like Bobbie Ann Mason. I am not trying to make up for the past. Nor is this, as one colleague sincerely but alarmingly misunderstood it, an attempt to help students to find their "inner child" and nurture its emergent literacy. I read to my students because I want them to experience how reading can be a shared as well as a solitary activity. As for the parents in my classes, I campaign hard to get them to read to their children. I encourage them to set that as one of their personal goals for the class, and a section of my class library is devoted to children's books they can borrow. These parents, many of them very young, have not made the connection between reading to children, modeling reading themselves, and seeing their children become readers. Yet all the parents I have taught hope that their children will "do better" in school than they did. They are not hard to sell on this idea of reading to their kids, once they try it.

Settling In

The first two weeks of workshop were trial and error. My initial minilessons were procedural, as Nancie Atwell suggests (1987, 129–30)—the rules for workshop participation, for example (basically students must be reading or writing letters during class). I did a lesson on what to write about in literary letters, namely anything related to reading or the students' books. Twice I did minilessons on how to exchange letters with one another and with me and how to safekeep them. Rather than repeat Atwell, let me refer you to her for this type of practical information. I simply lifted everything I did (and most of what I still do) from *In the Middle*. In Appendix

A, however, having caved into pressure from my peers, I have included my most recent course syllabus, to give you ideas for how you might go about running and grading a college workshop course. I have also included a reasonably descriptive list of many of the minilessons I use (Appendix B). While I would like to be cooperative and include more of the actual minilessons my colleagues and I use, the truth is we have stolen them from so many different places that we have no idea whom to credit.

By the end of the second week of classes, workshop was running itself. A typical class began when the students started arriving, usually around 8:50 A.M. Their first order of business, after updating one another on all that had transpired in their lives during the past twenty-four eventful hours, was to rearrange the furniture. How I envy primary and secondary teachers who have their own classrooms. My nephew David's kindergarten teacher, Ms. Phillips of Angleton, Texas, has an old claw-foot bathtub filled with pillows in her classroom so that her kids can "read in the tub," just like all over-the-top readers. But given the classroom shortage this institution faces, I would be handed a blindfold just for asking. Anyway, my students had to transform a highly institutional classroom, with bare walls, thirty student desks, weak fluorescent lights, and cell-like windows well above eye level, into a room that was comfortable for reading. They did remarkably well by taking matters into their own hands.

Each morning the students dismantled the neatly arranged rows in which the custodians had left their desks and established what I thought of as neighborhoods. Those who preferred solitude usually dragged their desks to the front of the room and angled themselves away from others. These folks were after the rural-route effect, where one's nearest neighbor was three miles away. The more social creatures arranged their desks into sloppy half or full circles near the back of the room. They rested their feet on the rungs of one another's chairs. If a student handed the person next to him a letter to pass to a person three desks away, the letter would be read by every student whose hands it passed through. This group reminded me of my neighborhood, where gossip rules and we sit on our stoops on summer nights because we find talking with and about each other far more interesting than television. A third group "borrowed" a sofa from a remote lounge in the building and, much to my surprise, it was not removed from the classroom. The four or five students who piled onto this battered yellow couch were nothing less than fraternity/ sorority row. This group was pleased with themselves, maybe for having the nerve to take the couch (which no one else ever attempted to sit on) or for having the fastest mouths in the class or for being the "wild" ones. No young adult novels for this crew. They read books about other rebels. I loved this group. Had I been in this class instead of teaching it, I would have been on the couch every day. Another "neighborhood" the class established was the smoker's ghetto. Smoking was permitted then (not now) in a lounge area across from the classroom, and the four smokers left for the lounge once the minilesson and status of the class were completed. I joined them once in awhile, to pass a literary letter or just to see how they were doing. The last small group of students sat or stretched out on the floor, in the middle of the room. They maintained their distance from one another, about two feet, but loaned each other pens and paper, as needed, and shared food. I thought of this group as the suburbs. Contact was casual and everyone wanted just enough room in which to sprawl. I doubt it will surprise you that the door to my classroom was always kept shut. No point in arousing the curiosity of idle colleagues.

I generally arrived as students were settling in, and what I brought with me each day was a library book cart filled with books. I figure blowing out a knee is only a matter of time, since I push around a two-hundred-pound book cart every day. Since I had to share the classroom and could not be assured that an in-class library would be secure, I came up with the idea of using a book cart I could take with me and then return to my office after each class. Workshop may not require an in-class library, but it helps to have a couple of hundred books at your disposal when you are trying to help a student decide what to read. Once the Learning Assistance Program had institutionalized the reading workshop approach, we purchased a fleet of these book carts so every teacher could have one. Have literature, will travel. I get a lot of business from people other than my students, too, as I ride up and down elevators with the cart, making suggestions and loaning books to colleagues and undergraduates.

The first time I taught workshop, the two hundred books on my cart were an assortment of my own books, as well as those donated by well-wishing colleagues. The majority were paperbacks, many badly worn, and they pretty much reflected that none of us had any idea what these students might want to read. I had four copies of *A Separate Peace* and six of *To Kill a Mockingbird*. Actually, Mary Ann Weiss, a colleague who taught writing, had given me all of her daughter Jessie's *Sweet Valley High* and Stephen King books, and this alone saved me that first semester. In Chapter 4, I discuss the kinds of books I learned to buy, but let me go ahead and explain my current system for acquiring books. First, I ask the institution for money to purchase books and get turned down. Then I once again rely on the kindness of far too literary friends and colleagues. Only now, instead of putting their donated books on my cart, I swap them for mass market paperbacks at a couple of good used book stores in the area. Since my students do not have to purchase books for the course, I also ask them each to contribute $10 to a book fund, which usually gives us about $200 to work with. I spend about $50 to $75 the first week of classes, buying current bestsellers I expect students will like, and then we go on a field trip to a downtown Cincinnati bookstore during the sixth or seventh week of the course. Students buy whatever they want until the money runs out. These books generally stay with the class library, but I lose about twenty books each semester, so I must constantly replace hot titles.

The first semester of workshop my class started at 9 A.M., and that is when I began the minilesson. After the first two weeks, these lessons included topics like knowing when to abandon a book, the reading process, prediction, the fictional curve, narrative structure, book awards, or oral reading—anything and everything I thought might be relevant. This lesson was from week 4:

"We've talked about how your knowledge of language allows you to predict what words and even whole sentences are getting at without noticing every single letter," I said, standing in the front of the room. "Well, we also predict what will happen next in a book, based on what we've read so far. Since we know how books work and how people act, we can form reasonable predictions. Then we read to see if we were right. Right now, Holly's reading a book called *April Fools.*" I walked over to the couch, where Holly sat squeezed into a middle position. "Holly, tell everybody what you told me about the book in your last letter."

"Want me to stop where I stopped in the letter?" she asked. "I've gotten past that part."

"Yeah, stop there."

"Uh, these three kids was riding around one night and they run this other car off the road," Holly said to the class, rather than to me. "They figured nobody could've survived the accident, so they kept going. But then Belinda, this one girl, got this weird doll's head in the mail. She wondered if it had something to do with the accident. Then she starts tutoring this boy who missed school because he was in a car accident. Is that where I got to?"

"Yeah," I said, looking around the room. "So what do ya'll think is going to happen next in this book?"

"It's a horror-type book?" Dave wanted to know.

Holly held up the book to show the cover, which pictured a bloody knife and a severed doll's head sticking out of a mailbox. "I picked it because it looked like a horror."

Dave drummed his fingers on his desk. "I think this guy she's tutoring was the one she ran off the road. He's pissed and just waiting to get her back."

"Can't be a coincidence," Mac volunteered from his seat in the suburbs, "her tutoring a guy who's been in a wreck and all."

"I think she'll fall in love with him," LeeAnn said, "then he'll scare the shit out of her to get even."

Rebecca looked at Holly and said, "They should've stopped and seen if they could help."

I moved to stand beside Rebecca. "That'd make it a morality tale. That's one of the oldest plots in the world. If they had only done the right thing, none of this awful stuff would have happened to them, right?" I pointed toward Rebecca. "You used something you know about how stories work to take a guess at the point of this story. LeeAnn, why'd you predict they'd fall in love?"

"'Cause it'll be ten times worse when she finds out who he really is. It'd make the story better."

"You guys ever think about writing these things?" I said to no one in particular. "Holly, you'll have to let us know what does happen."

Holly said, "I can tell you now that LeeAnn is sorta close, but so are Dave and Mac."

"One thing's for sure," Dave said. "Somebody'll get cut. Holly hasn't read a book yet where somebody doesn't get hacked to pieces."

"Just getting some tips for when I go after you," Holly said, smiling sweetly.

I laughed. "Anyway, in my literary letters, I'm going to ask you to predict what happens next in your book. And what I'm trying to do with that is to keep you sorting through what you already know about the book, the details of the plot, the foreshadowing, all the hints, as well as what you know about books in general and how people behave, and see how you would put it together for somebody who hasn't read the book."

And on another day, I drew the fictional curve on the board, telling students that rising action, which was full of obstacles for the characters, led to the climax, which, when resolved, led to the falling action. I explained that some stories did not follow this structure but that most did. Then I continued:

"So Ray, you're reading a play called *That Championship Season*. What's the rising action in that? Who are the characters and why did they get together?" I went and sat beside Ray in his secluded post at the front of the room, having a conversation with him the others were invited to listen to.

"Well, they're these old guys who played on their high school basketball team a long time ago, and they get together every year to celebrate their championship game. They're living in the past."

"Okay, so these guys just want to get together and feel like heroes," I said. "Any obstacles?"

Ray nodded. "They all get drunk and start acting like assholes—sorry." He put his hand over his mouth for a moment.

"A rose by any other name, Ray. So they were acting like assholes and . . .?"

"And they start talking . . . stuff about one guy sleeping with another guy's wife. And another guy's business is a failure. They get more obnoxious, so you know they'll end up fighting."

"And is that the conflict? They start punching each other?"

"Not exactly. But you know, it does build up to a climax, like you said. They tell worse and worse secrets, until this one guy says that they cheated to win the championship game. They deliberately injured this other player. So it's out. They're cheaters, not champions."

"What's the resolution?"

"I think they all see what a bunch of losers they are. But then the party's over and they go back to pretending they have a life."

"Ray, you're brilliant, thank you," I said and stood up. "In your letters, or just in your heads, you might try to map out your books to see if they fit this pattern. And if you're reading a book that doesn't fit, tell me about that, too."

The minilesson was always followed by what Nancie Atwell calls a "status of the class conference" (1987, 89–92), or check, during which I asked each student what he or she was reading or working on that day. Lucy and Vivian were the only students who read during status of the class. The others listened in while locating pens, browsing the book cart, or checking their folders for new mail. By the time I did status of the class, I had moved to the center of the room, where I would later sit on the floor with students. I went down the roll and wrote down the title of each student's book on a simple form I had devised:

"Lynn? What are you working on today?"

"I'm reading *Dear Sister*."

"Mimi?"

"I finished *Brian's Girl* on Friday and *Christy's Love* over the weekend. Now I'm reading *Racing Hearts*."

"Jesus," Dave said. "I hate going after her. I did not finish *Fear and Loathing in Las Vegas* over the weekend, and I won't finish it by next weekend either."

"Jerry, how about you," I asked.

"*Presumed Innocent*, but I'm thinking of abandoning it."

"That's fine. What don't you like?"

"It doesn't make sense. Stuff like this doesn't happen to guys like Rusty. It's not realistic. I don't think I like fiction," Jerry finished.

I turned to Lance, who was at the book cart. "Looking for a new book?" He nodded in the affirmative.

"Joanie?"

"*Class Pictures*, still."

"Ray? You're reading the Bible, right?"

"Like that would be on *your* book cart. *Death of a Salesman*," Ray said and held up his well-worn copy.

"You know he got Cliff Notes for it, don't you?" Dave said.

37

"Shut up, Dave. Ray is an extraordinary reader with an acute critical sensibility," I said. "Holly?"

"*Rage of Angels*, but I have to write a letter first."

"Jackie?"

"Guess."

"Could it be . . . *War Day*?"

The remainder of the class (about forty minutes) was spent reading or writing and exchanging literary letters. During the semester in which I conducted my research, I generally read for about ten minutes, to help students get settled, and then began writing field notes. Now I read along with students throughout the entire workshop. The first few minutes were always tense for me, as the students decided what kind of day it was going to be. There was always some initial shuffling and settling, as students got themselves organized, but within a few minutes the entire class had generally eased into an absorbed and oblivious silence. They were *gone*, off with their pirates and mass murderers. My signal to end class, forty minutes later, was to ask if students had any letters for me, and the sound of my voice startled some as they made their dazed way back into the real world. Now that I read along with students, my experience is similar, and when they tell me this is the most relaxing part of their week, I tell them the same is true for me.

Holly, Kelly, and Sara were walking back to my office with me one day after class when Holly said, "I'm glad I have this class after math. I get a sick stomach in math. I never understand anything, and we have a test every week. But I feel better as soon as I start reading."

"That happens for me when I read at home too," Kelly said. "My stepmom can ream me out about how useless I am, and I'll go up to my room and start reading. What's cool is she sees me reading and knows she isn't getting to me."

The many uses of literacy.

While reading and writing went smoothly and productively most of the time, there were days when the students were restless. They ripped pages out of their notebooks, ransacked their backpacks, coughed or sighed, and stretched or yawned. No one was deliberately disruptive, but one or two antsy students could get under everyone's skin. I would find myself reading the same paragraph three times, unable to focus. A look around the room suggested we were all having the same problem. The students would read, then stop to write letters, then stop that and start reading again. Nothing seemed to work. On days like that, my only relief came from knowing that students were also reading outside class.

I loved to watch students read, but I had to be surreptitious; otherwise, they sensed my attention and raised their eyes, which broke their concentration. Jerry and Valerie read with their books inches away from their eyes. Mac held his book with the front cover folded over, one hand holding the book and the other propping up his chin. Jackie read laying fully prone, head propped on her backpack, the book held in the air. When Lance read *The Frontiersman*, a long and bulky tome, I could see him struggle to keep the book open until I suggested he break the spine by folding the book back on itself. I haven't much room to talk, since I am a compulsive foot jiggler, but Mimi and LeeAnn had turbocharged feet. One or the other of them would sit with her stationary foot on Mac's desk, the other churning air. I heard him whisper to Mimi, "If I wanted Magic Fingers I'd have put a quarter in the machine." One student moved his lips as he read, occasionally subvocalizing. Ray was a reading contortionist the likes of which I have never seen since. He held his book in his lap and rested his forehead on the top of his student desk. Mac sometimes listened to recordings of books on a personal cassette player, and read along with the print copy. The volume on his tape player was turned up loud enough one day that a tinny sound could be heard throughout the room. Kelly said, "Do I get credit for reading Mac's book too, since I can hear it?" Mac missed the entire exchange, but the rest of us were amused. Such interruptions of the whole class were rare, but always funny. I think the students knew it had better be good (i.e., make me laugh) if they were going to halt everyone's reading and writing. While students generally did not speak during workshop, I responded to personal conversations with the reminder, "You need to be reading or writing."

Students were free to eat or drink during workshop. Mountain Dew, which could launch the space shuttle with its equal parts sugar and caffeine, was the beverage of choice, except for those of us over twenty-one, who preferred coffee. And maybe I should hit up Kellogg's for a couple of hundred new books, since my students consumed Rice Krispy marshmallow treats by the square acre that semester. These were sold at a vending cart in the lobby of the building, along with chocolate-covered chocolate donuts, another comfort food that seemed indispensable when it came to students' reading. Oh, and nacho cheese-flavored Doritos, a veritable arsenal of artificial ingredients, also seemed to make reading that much easier for my students. I was in awe about just how much food a fit and trim eighteen-year-old male could consume in an hour. I am serious, although quite possibly off the deep end, when I suggest that grazing made it easier and more pleasant for students to read. Lots of people need external gratification for pursuing difficult tasks. I know I never would have skied down Big Mountain in Montana during a whiteout so dense I could not tell if I were standing still or moving if I had not been reminded by a companion that I could drink Heineken in the lodge all night if only I abandoned my plan to lay down in the snow and wait for death. The ends, since we are not talking anything truly evil like heroin or plagiarism, justified the means. Whatever made it easier for my students to read was fine by me.

Students also wrote letters in class, as well as at home. They consulted their books as they wrote their letters, thumbing back and forth through the pages. The usual means of delivering mail was to put a letter in a classmate's folder—

folders were kept in alphabetical order on the book cart—and to hand over letters written to me directly. Dave, however, always folded his letters into paper airplanes and, announcing "Airmail," sent them flying across the room in the vicinity of the addressee. Students wrote their letters on various types of paper, everything from stationery to college-ruled notebook paper. That first workshop, I wrote my response letters on legal pads, but I eventually adopted the students' idea of using stationery. Since responding to students' letters is very time-consuming, and I type faster than I can write by hand, I now use a computer to write my responses, but I print out the letters on the most colorful and creative paper I can find.

At the moment, I am trying to rid myself of all paper, cute or otherwise, in order to make my way through *virtual* rain, sleet, snow, and dead of night. In other words, I want to be able to exchange literary letters with my students via electronic mail. This is not Stanford, so none of my students own PCs and modems, but with my Macintosh Powerbook, a modem, and a dedicated phone line, I can establish an Internet link in my classroom. Outside class, my students can use Northern's computer lab and, with any luck or some persistent whining, our writing center will also go on-line for convenient e-mail access. Imagine how this would work. Students could send me or their classmates literary letters as often as they liked, day or night, not just when we were in class. Responses would be immediate, rather than governed by when the class met. I suspect the "letters" would be briefer, more frequent, and more spontaneous, since that is how e-mail works in my professional and personal experience, but the immediacy of sending and receiving e-mail makes for a greater sense of dialogue than does snail mail (the US Postal Service) or, I suspect, the three-times-a-week pick-up and delivery of workshop mail.

I think the novelty of e-mail alone would produce prolific correspondence between students, as well as between students and me. And I think e-mail is an intoxicating way to introduce the powers of computing to students, even the two-fingered typists like me. Think about it. You log-in after lunch, check your mail, and find six new messages from classmates. You write back to a couple of them. At four, you log in again and write back to a couple more. If you are wired up at home, you can write back to the other two after dinner. Or, if you like, you can save the messages and write back once or twice a week. Personally, I like the idea that my students could reach me any time inspiration struck, and I would have the option of responding immediately, if I were not otherwise engaged, or at my leisure. They too could choose to respond whenever they were ready. And think about the potential of free and instant communication via e-mail. One day, my students will be able to exchange literary letters with another workshop class, at another college, in another state. Great balls of fire. Just think about the kinds of audience awareness this kind of exchange might require and therefore exercise. Any takers? E-mail me at my Internet address, "HENRY@NKU.EDU."

Back to what was, instead of what will be. The only major break in the workshop routine came during a field trip to a bookstore. These field trips are a regular and favorite part of my workshops. They vary little. About six weeks into the semester, I propose to a class that we take a field trip to a bookstore in downtown Cincinnati. I am met with considerable resistance, because the students are afraid of getting lost, not knowing "how to act," and of having difficulty parking in downtown. They want to go to a chain bookstore in a familiar suburban mall. But I am not interested in taking them to a bookstore that sells more calendars than books and has only new releases, so, sensitive teacher that I am, I ignore them. We usually stay in the bookstore about an hour and a half, before we spend all of our money and are in overload anyway. We browse, talk about books, and show each other our purchases. I always call the store, Brentano's, to explain that I will be descending with eighteen students, so they will not be alarmed (that is a tip, by the way). The staff, sympathetic to my goal of promoting reading, goes out of their way to chat with the students about books and authors, to recommend titles, and to explain the layout of the store. The students love the VIP treatment, and I love seeing them receive it. Afterward, we walk around downtown, window shopping, discussing such things as whether or not we are willing to dress for success, and how cool we think it is that women can now wear sensible shoes to and from the office, even though Nikes look funny with London Fog trench coats. I twist a few arms and the class decides to have lunch at an ethnic restaurant, often Chinese, rather than McDonald's. Fortune cookies make for a great literary experience, as well as a tasty mini-lesson on not believing everything you read.

Reading workshop is a moveable feast, since all we need is our books, and I like to roam. So as soon as the weather at our windy hilltop campus permits, I am the first to suggest that the class adjourn to the great outdoors to read. There is a pond on campus called Lake Inferior, and this is an ideal spot for what is, in my mind only, a Walden experience. After the bitter winter we experienced during that first workshop, my students were desperate to enjoy a perfect and early spring. We shifted electric wheelchairs into manual, pushed our classmates down to the pond, donned our Ray-Bans, sat on the lush green grass or on benches, and read. For me, the view was breathtaking—students making use of one of the few natural spots on an imposingly modern campus to read books that they had chosen and were enjoying. We swatted flies, squealed at persistent bees, and stared up at a perfectly blue sky. I think these glory days of delighting in fair weather, in reading, and in being together went a long way in expanding my students' sense of what reading was or could be. For me, reading workshop will always be associated with the pure pleasure of seeing students read without protest.

The final measure I used with the class was a mandatory, standardized course-and-instructor evaluation instrument developed by the university. Students were asked to assign numerical values (1–5, with 5 being highest) to various aspects of course and instructor effectiveness. My attitude toward students, my enthusiasm, and my ability were each rated 4.92 (university means: 4.24, 4.08, and 4.33, respectively). Students gave me an overall evaluation of 5.0 (university mean: 4.15), and rated how much they had learned in the course as 4.64 (university mean: 4.03). Their overall evaluation of the course was 4.92 (university mean: 3.92). But who knows what these results really mean? Maybe I told more jokes than the average professor, or better ones. Maybe the class was less stressful than most, or perhaps I gave better grades. The only really useful question on the evaluation asked, "Has your interest in the subject changed as a result of this course?" These are the comments the students made: "I've started reading more." "I learned a lot about reading." "[The course] got me to read more." "I have become a reader." "Reading seems much easier." "Would like to take [the course] again." "I enjoyed reading much more when I got to pick my own books to read." "I thought [the course] was going to be stupid but it wasn't." "Yes, I really enjoy reading."

The only trouble with temptation is that it is so, you know, tempting. The quantitative data I collected from the Nelson-Denny and the course/instructor evaluation, which were normal class procedures rather than efforts to assess the effectiveness of workshop, could be trotted out as evidence that reading workshop improves students' reading ability. But not so fast. First, who said anything about improving students' reading ability? I did not adopt the workshop approach because I thought it would make students better readers in fifteen weeks. My goal was to make them willing, if not habitual, readers by giving them an opportunity to explore a fuller range of literacy experiences. It was willing and frequent practice, over time, that I bet on as the only means of improving reading. Maybe the course improved students' ability, but you cannot "prove" it by me or by my data—it was not that kind of study and not that kind of course. Second, I am convinced that the Nelson-Denny, if it measures anything useful at all, measures a type of reading different from the one I taught. Students in every reading workshop I have taught, until I abandoned Nelson-Denny testing a year ago, have achieved similar gains.

Chapter 4

Buckets O' Blood

I know you have had that teacher dream, or some variation of it, that goes like this. You get a heart-stopping piece of news on the last day of the semester: there is this class you were supposed to have been teaching all along. Twenty angry students, who have been waiting something along the line of three months for you to show up, are more than eager to hear you explain this one, preferably in the presence of the provost and the press. The fat lady is singing, and "Loser" is the name of her tune. Then you wake up. Sure, you are sweat-soaked and tangled in the sheets, but your career is intact. It was only a dream. Now imagine yourself standing in front of a group of nonreaders and telling them the goal of your course is for them to find books they will love. You say you will help with them with this, and you mean it. But then a student asks if you can recommend a good ghost story, and Toni Morrison's *Beloved* is the one and only book that pops into your head. Somebody else wants a book about fishing. So what are you going to recommend, *Moby Dick*? Only this was not a dream.

When I began teaching workshop, I had never read a novel by Danielle Steel, Stephen King, or Michael Crichton. Dean R. Koontz and Jude Devereaux were unknown to me. I did not object to these books, I was just oblivious to most of what got written and read by the millions of people around me. I did not know that V. C. Andrews was dead. I thought S. E. Hinton was a man. What was Richard Bachman to Stephen

47

King? Alter ego? Evil twin? Forget about it. That first semester, I was nearly useless when it came to helping my students find books to read. I did not know how to make recommendations based on their interests, and I had no idea how to encourage them to read strategically, since I knew next to nothing about what they *were* reading, let alone what that signaled they *could* be reading with a little informed encouragement. How did I fail to see this coming? Did I think that my students were going to read *The New York Times Review of Books?* I tell you, as a reading teacher, I was very out of touch with reading.

What to Read?

During that first class, I was stunned by the array of titles my students trotted out during the status-of-the-class check. Those eighteen students read a total of one hundred and thirty-three books, including ninety-three different titles, and of those, I had read only fifteen. Who were these authors? And wait a minute, I was the expert, so where and how were students finding these books of which I had never heard? I knew I was missing something about popular literature, left out of some loop, so I started asking. That first semester, when Kelly came to class with *The Original Book of the Dead*, about the band, I asked how she had come across it. She replied, "I was over at this friend's house and it was sitting on her coffee table. I said, Hey I want to read that, and then I thought, Hey I have to read for class anyhow. This is too perfect. It was cosmic."

Not everyone's planets were so perfectly aligned as Kelly's, so I asked Jackie how she had found a book called *War Day*. I learned of her friend Bridget, an avid reader who kept Jackie supplied. "I'm her project," Jackie wrote. "She's been trying to get me to read books she likes all through high school." Whenever Jackie needed a book, she and Bridget put their heads together until they came up with something. Bridget quickly became an *ex officio* member of the class. Not only did Jackie refer to Bridget regularly in her letters to me, telling me what Bridget thought about the books Jackie was reading, Bridget also passed on her suggestions to Jackie's friends in the class. She even visited twice and read with us. Bridget, where are you now? I see a workshop compatriot in the making. In my years of reading workshop, there have been dozens of Bridgets. These very odd friends who, as Jackie incredulously wrote, "would rather read than party" are even more precious to a workshop teacher than the collected works of Stephen King.

What I have learned in subsequent workshop classes is that it is mothers who provide most of the out-of-class recommendations on which students follow through. All these years, Mama has been slipping off to read novels of true crime, horror, suspense, mystery, and romance. Beloved son or daughter only notices this when he or she is (a) hungry, (b) in need of the car keys, or (c) desperate for a book to read for my class. I like to cross-fertilize, so when a student reads a book his or her mother has recommended, I often ask if I can borrow it. And in many situations, this has led to a literary-letter correspondence between me and Mama, which I begin with a thank-you note for letting me borrow the book. Before you know it, Mama and I are plotting about Junior's reading. As one mother wrote:

> James read Jurassic Park after I told him about it. I'm glad you liked it too. Can you think of other books I should buy to keep him interested in reading? All we ever talk about is where are you going? Who are you going with? But we talked about the book and saw the movie together. We haven't shared this much since he turned thirteen. Plus I know his grades will improve if he gets in the habit of reading.

Can I get a witness? Reading means more than success in school. It is also a bridge between people, a point of contact, or simply having something to say. For every parent who has ever wondered why one of my students was "wasting" his or her time with a book, there has been a parent whose under-standing of what reading can bring to a person's life far exceeds the pragmatic, academically oriented, and norm-referenced expectations of our field.

Before reading workshop, I regarded cable TV merely as a means of viewing fifty channels of crap instead of the four to five you would receive by simply plugging in your set. But the "infomercials" on late-night cable TV have been good to me by providing my self-helpers with a steady supply of reading material. Kim described her discovery of a book called *Wealth Without Risk*:

> I was watching TV late one night last week and they had a short segment on that was about this man Charles J. Givens. At first I wasn't really paying much attention. All of a sudden, I found myself glued to the TV listening to what he was talking about, and I'm glad I did.

I have exchanged literary letters with students about how to buy real estate with no down payment, how to soothe one's inner child, how to love less or how to love more, as well as how to dress for success. I can barely stand to read or to dis-cuss these books, but they go with the turf.

Naturally, students get recommendations from one an-other about what to read, but I have been lucky enough on several occasions to see "cohorts" of readers form within a class. During that first semester, Mimi was the diva, the dar-ling, and maybe even the demon of a group of teen romance readers that included LeeAnn, Lynn, Hiroko, and sometimes Mac. As soon as Mimi finished a book, she passed it on to LeeAnn, who then passed it to Hiroko, who finally handed it over to Lynn. The four women wrote letters to one another, and although I did not formally study students' intercorre-spondence, I read through their letters to one another and noticed that Mimi instructed her gang on what they should like about the books she recommended and what might be learned from them. Mimi handed several books directly to

Mac instead of running them through the loop since, as she informed me, he had "special needs." I asked what she meant, and she replied, "He needs books where the shy guy gets the girl. The girls want to read about the kind of guy who can sweep you off your feet, but I think those books would make him feel bad."

Now that I have a sense of how students go about finding books, I do a minilesson very early in the semester about the utility of getting better acquainted with those geek kids from high school who always had their noses in books, or asking Mama just what novel had her so tied up in knots that she burned the Rice-a-Roni. I point out that snooping around a friend's bookshelf is not only a good way to find out if this is someone you should date, but also a fine way of locating books you might want to borrow and read. And I encourage those students who are never at a loss for something to read to take their classmates under their wing by making recommendations.

Reading over Their Shoulders

The way I looked at it that first semester, I had a lot of catching up to do. I read very nearly every book a student recommended to me, which added up to seventeen titles. Sure, I hated romance novels, but they appealed to some of my students, so I read them. I was honest with them that romance was not my favorite genre, but this only led romance fans to work twice as hard to find books that would win me over. And despite all those brooding looks and heaving bosoms, my students' excitement carried me through the reading. Before I knew it, I was hooked on most types of popular literature, and I still read fifteen to twenty books my students recommend each semester. I continue to read the esoteric books I prefer, but not in class. Try discussing *Love in the Time of Cholera* with a peer, let alone exchanging a literary letter about it with someone who is trying to make the transition from *TV Guide* to Stephen King. Honest, it feels like you are insulting someone's intelligence, even if you are not sure whose.

I am leading up to something here. Others might be better able to blend their more literary reading into workshop than I was, but I still think workshop teachers have to commit to reading what their students do. First, you need to know your audience and your product. Workshop teachers are selling reading. Second, if you exclusively read books that your students find inaccessible, you may be telling them that they are not yet fully fledged readers, that it is the book, rather than the act of reading, that determines such things. The message may be that there are high-minded readers, such as yourself, who would never lower themselves to read the kind of visceral and gratifying "trash" students do. In my opinion, calling a book "trash" is only a breath away from calling its reader "trash," but I have heard the term nastily applied to the books I "let" my students read. As a workshop teacher, if you cannot make yourself read what your students do—even a real stomach-turner about Jeffrey Dahmer—then you consign yourself to learning less than you could and knowing less than you will need to about your students' reading.

As I said, workshop teachers are selling reading. So, think back about the salespersons you have encountered. Have you ever gone into a store and gotten a hard sell from some uppity clerk to buy an item you simply could not afford? You know how that feels. Only a loser would or could not buy the product. Think about how our students feel if we consistently try to sell them books that are too difficult, too foreign, or too uninteresting to them. Salespersons are motivated by commission, but we might be motivated by a different sort of capital. It would be juicy, yes, to brag that our neoliterates are reading Milan Kundera, and trust me, you can sell any student on the first ten pages of any book. But unlike the clerk, who is not around when the bills come due, workshop teachers can see the consequences of their failed recommendations.

Students willingly abandon books that are too difficult, but they feel badly when they do, especially if the book is one the teacher said was good. We need to be able to offer what our customers need.

Surely you have also had the experience of going into a store to buy an item and not getting the help you need. Say you want to buy a bicycle that doubles for touring and off-road riding. The teenage clerk, who only ends his phone conversation when it looks like you are about to take a bicycle chain and whack him over the head with it, saunters over, and says, "You need help or something?" By this time, the help you need is a beta-blocker, but you calmly and, with the benefit of a doubt, ask if the bicycle before you will do the job. The answer you receive is, "I don't know. I don't ride. I just work here." The frustration of someone contemplating spending six hundred dollars on a bicycle is probably about the same as that of a student contemplating devoting twenty hours to reading *The Firm* when his teacher's reply to his query about the book is, "I don't know, dear. I haven't read it." In other words, *I just work here . . . and read National Book Award winners.* In workshop, we are not just there to run the register and to record sales. We have to be there to provide fully informed assistance.

By reading what my students read, I become a part of the community that forms within the class. I am in on things. I can sit back with the other ten students who have read *The Bridges of Madison County* and exchange knowing glances as we watch a classmate read the last chapter and wait for her to start crying. I know what part of Jerry Seinfeld's *SeinLanguage* a student is just about to lose it over, and I know where the sexy bits are in the novels of Anne Rice. And I know why so many students start Stephen King's *Cujo* only to abandon it. When Sondra and Cheryl recently suggested a class boycott of John Grisham's *A Time to Kill* because they thought the book was racist, I understood what they were talking about only because I had read the book. I was also able to stop the near fistfight that erupted between them and the

Grisham fans by means of an instant minilesson on how the meaning of that book, like any other, is negotiable.

Students' literary letters give me a road map for purposefully reading along with them. During an early workshop class, for example, Nikki said that Danielle Steel's *Secrets* was confusing her: "It just mixes me up. The characters seem to change names or something." Nikki had been told that she was learning disabled, and while she had been very pleased with herself for selecting a long book, she finally got discouraged. "I guess this is my first and last book. I am a worse reader than I thought." I swooped into the bookstore after class, bought a copy of *Secrets*, and read it before the next class. What confused Nikki (and dozens of subsequent students) was a multiple-point-of-view narrative. Once I told Nikki how the book worked, she was fine. How else would I have learned that many of my students are thrown by something as standard as point-of-view shifts?

Although Alice Walker's *Possessing the Secret of Joy* was not a book I had to make myself read, it provides another example of a near miss avoided only because I had already read a book a student selected. I thought the book was too difficult for my freshmen, so when Angela brought a copy with her to class, I wondered how she would fare with it. And, in fact, it was not too long before I heard, "I'm not understanding this book at all. I'm all confused." I guessed she was having trouble with Walker's use of two names for the main character. But no, Angela informed me that Walker "uses Tashi when her more African thoughts are in her mind and Evelyn when she's thinking like an American." Damn. That was good. But Angela finally told me after class one day that she was going to give up on the book.

"You wouldn't believe what I thought it was about," Angela said.

"Tell me."

She leaned close, cupped her hand over her mouth and whispered in my ear.

"But Angela," I said. "That *is* what the book's about."

"Oh my sweet Jesus," she said. "Tashi's gonna have to kill somebody for that. She's gonna kill that old woman in Africa, isn't she? And maybe that dictator guy too. That's it, isn't it?"

"Good, you're predicting, but you know I never tell how a book ends."

"I'll finish it by Monday. Then we'll see just how right I am."

For the record and since I am always asked, I never say anything negative or dismissive about a book a student recommends to me. Admittedly, I have had to think very hard sometimes for something complimentary to say about a book in which a woman is stalked and then mutilated before the author turns his attention to the "brilliant" pathology of the killer. Pat O'Reilly, one of my dissertation committee members, asked me during my defense how I managed to rein in my own reaction to some of the books my students read. A good question. My answer is that I have situational integrity. In the women's studies courses I teach, I serve up moral indignation baked, broiled, and fried about the way violence against women is portrayed as entertaining in the media. But in reading workshop, I am just grateful my students will read. My principles shift with my priorities. I have celebrated buckets full of blood and super jumbo body counts with the best of them.

The way I see it, you have to have your finger on the pulse in workshop. And the only way I know how to tell you to do that is to read along with your students. It may be easy for me, since my smart, expert, and mouthy colleagues never took me the least bit seriously in the first place—so I have no face to lose by reading thrillers and chillers—but in workshop, preparing for class means reading a number of books you might not otherwise elect to read. Oh, but tell me you *wanted* to read the college reading textbook you used to assign? And, okay, I will admit that I read at the speed of light, but that is mostly because I know the art of skimming and skipping in formula fiction. So do you. You can read the first and last thirty pages of any romance novel and know all you need to to hold an informed discussion with a student. You can read and comprehend Dean R. Koontz dead drunk, and once you have read a V. C. Andrews novel, you can read every fifth page of the next one and sound like an expert. Take any shortcuts your time and taste dictate, but do your homework. The reward is seeing your students do theirs.

What Students Will Read

When O. J. Simpson's ex-wife and her friend were murdered, the evidence suggested that Simpson did everything but sign his name to the crime. This business is no laughing matter, since two people are dead, but to an opportunistic workshop teacher, this tragedy also means great stuff. This story has it all. First, the books written about (and *by!*) Simpson fit the true-crime genre, a favorite among my readers, and second, the subject of these books is not only a celebrity, he is an *athlete*. It does not get better than this. I am not without shame, but I believe that critical reading does not require a critical text, it requires critical thinking. Workshop's literary letters allow me to ask students questions about their reading that go beyond Simpson's guilt, or the details of the case, or the troubled childhood that undoubtedly will be unearthed. I can ask students whether or not they could have served as uninformed and unbiased members of his jury, given the media exposure the case received. I can ask why the media is focusing on everything Simpson threw away—fame, money, and freedom—rather than on what he allegedly took away—human life. In my experience with literary letters, if you put a wiggly worm in the water, you will get a bite.

Books that are hot one semester are likely to be about as appealing as tooth decay the next. O. J., along with Tonya, Nancy, and Lorena, are good for just a few months. Then it is time to keep an ear to the ground for the next scandal or tragedy that will grab the public's attention. My students, like mainstream readers in general, are primarily interested in what is new, whether they are reading fiction or fact. Check out chain bookstores like Waldenbooks and B. Dalton, and you will see that these retailers appreciate the public taste and stock only the newest releases for most authors. This means that I have to keep reading. I also have to keep buying books. My Simpson collection will either have to go to used bookstores or to the recycling bin, unless I decide to store them until the inevitable made-for-TV movie, when the flames of interest will once again be fanned. One thing that keeps workshop from getting stale after all these years is finding out what each new group of students will want to read.

When it comes to buying books my students will probably like, tabloid television is not my only source of inspiration. Hit films, far better publicized than the books from which they were derived, seize my students' attention. Once upon a time I used to arrive at movies late enough to miss the previews of coming attractions. I saw no point in sitting through commercials for movies I would never think of seeing, but now I consider the previews the best part. Last night I went to a movie that previewed John Grisham's *The Client.* I was restless throughout the feature, since I knew this best-yet adaptation of a Grisham novel would send my students straight through the roof. Not only would they love the book, the film would rekindle their interest in Grisham's older novels, just as the success of *Jurassic Park* the year before had my students reading everything Michael Crichton had ever written, clear back to *The Andromeda Strain.*

I think reading and literature teachers are a little hinky about the idea of students' reading books after they have seen films, given that I have been asked at least a hundred times how I know a student is reading a book when he or she could have just watched the movie. In answer, I see them read. We get together three times a week to read for forty minutes.

None of my students is so determined to avoid reading that he or she would or could sustain the kind of mindless, page-turning pretense it would take to fake reading. Sure, they are underprepared for college work, but they are not brain-dead. And I know you know what it would take to sustain this kind of ruse. Surely you too have pretended to read, in an airplane or in a doctor's office, in order to avoid the relentless bore in the next seat who simply will not let up. Pretending to read takes far more energy than reading does.

Some students want to read the book because they saw the movie. Others want to read it because they plan to see the movie. You can have great literary-letter exchanges about these preferences, too. I am in the read-first-see-later camp, but students will argue that since the book is generally better than the movie, they have more to look forward to if they see the film first and read later. But I wonder if there is more to it than that. We know that the more prior knowledge you have about a subject the more likely you are to understand what you read about it. Well, if you have seen an easily understandable film before reading the book, it seems to me that your reading is going to be much easier, virtually a guaranteed success. Success is good. It makes us all feel like a million.

Building a Library

Today, I went book buying with my colleague Wanda Crawford. We needed to replenish our own book carts, as well as to stock a couple of carts for part-time faculty new to the workshop. At Brentano's in downtown Cincinnati, where we enjoy a generous discount, Wanda cracked me up by holding up romances that practically quivered and saying, "So good, so good" in imitation of our students' highest praise of a book. Later, while Wanda looked at the science fiction and I was pulling multiple copies of John Grisham off the shelf, she turned to me and asked, "What should I get in the action adventure category?"

"Anything with an automatic weapon on the cover," I replied.

I was making rude noises about Wanda's selection of *Time Cop*, a novel about, you guessed it, a cop who travels through time, until the clerk happened to mention that Jean-Claude van Damme would be starring in the soon-to-be released film version. I literally abandoned the conversation midsentence to run over to the shelves to get a copy for my own cart. That Wanda knows what's up. Back in the office, we made a list of the fundamentals of a workshop collection to order through the university bookstore (see Appendix C), investing heavily in horror, suspense, romance, glamour romance, true crime, select legal thrillers, select science fiction/fact, and sports.

In the horror category, we selected the shortest Stephen King books, along with other favorites like Dean R. Koontz and John Saul. When I can see a book rather than just select it from a catalogue, I tend to go for anything with a bloody, clawed hand on the cover. Mutilation by a half-human beast provides that winning combination of being both fascinating and repellent. Workshop has taught me a deep appreciation of thrillers, and so Wanda deferred to me when it came to ordering books in that genre. Top of my list are books like Joy Fielding's *See Jane Run* and Nancy Price's *Sleeping with the Enemy*. My female students like these books because a victimized woman decides to fight back not with violence but with her wits. Novelizations of nerve-janglers like *Basic Instinct* and *Sliver* have a short shelf life, tied as they are to films that came and went, but whatever thrillers are playing in the theater ought to play well in a workshop library for a semester or so.

In the romance genre, Wanda said we should get Rosamond Pilcher, oh so good, you know. I nodded to her wisdom and added a couple of titles by Jude Devereaux, because in her books the protagonist's bosom is heaving not because she is writhing with passion but because she is laughing so hard. These lighthearted historical romances have real charm. LaVyrle Spencer, whom I call LaHurl in private, is another

romantic favorite. A few students enjoy Harlequin and Sil-
houette romances, but it is the glamour romances of Danielle
Steel and Judith Krantz that female students swoon over. Ah,
the *real* American dream: meeting a billionaire-who-just-
wants-to-be-loved-for-who-he-is. Read 'em and weep. On a
related note, any book reveling in conspicuous consumption,
as long as it does not lose students with knowing references
to Aubusson rugs and Porthault sheets, appeals to minimum-
wage earners who must count every nickel and dime.

In the true-crime genre, the most popular books involve
high-profile cases, obsessive greed, or really sick stuff. Much
of whatever is being featured on *A Current Affair* or *Hard
Copy* is a pretty safe workshop bet, but my students passed on
Joey Buttafucco. As one of them said to me at the time, "I
think the only reason that loser is in the news is because his
name sounds like a dirty word and they get off saying it on
TV." You probably *can* run a fine workshop without cultivat-
ing my newly found interest in the least uplifting elements of
society. I mean, I am well aware that I am the only person in
America, other than those owning the rights to a number of
books, who is looking forward to the twentieth anniversary of
the Jonestown tragedy in 1998. But students do love these
books, and they will read them by the dozen since they generally rate high on the gore score.

While we were out shopping today, Wanda also bought a
couple of science fiction titles for her classes, but this has
always been a dead genre among my students. As we talked
about what we were buying, Wanda and I concluded that our
personal preferences do shape some of what gets read in
workshop. My book cart, for example, has no science fiction,
since I cannot grasp the genre. Wanda, who is of a higher
moral caliber than me, is repulsed by true-crime books and so
has fewer of those. Her students read science fiction and mine
read true crime. Since I do not want to see my students
inherit my limitations, I have started reading science fiction
and am adding more out-of-this-world titles to my cart.

On the other hand, my students have not taken to the law-and-order novels I like so much. Other than the works of John Grisham, judicial thrillers generally do not play well among my students. One problem is that of the recent proliferation of lawyers-turned-writers, most tend to create thoroughly jaded central characters. My students dislike those who experience inner struggle. With Grisham's characters, self-interest is always an issue, but the good can readily be distinguished from the bad and, best yet, everyone gets what is coming. Authors like Scott Turow and Phillip Friedman reach for principles but, like Oscar Wilde, my students prefer persons to principles. They want to read about people who know this from that, not those who ponder the shades of gray. Try as I might, I cannot pass on my delight in these books.

Buying sports books is tough for me; Wanda too. I cannot name more than five professional athletes in either basketball, football, or baseball. And I think Michael and Magic are just about played out. My resolution for the next academic year is to get it together and start reading about professional sports. In the meantime, I quite accidentally learned that while biographies of sports figures are popular, so are books about technique, buying equipment, and officiating. I now buy books about in-line skating, skateboarding, bicycling, golf, and tennis. Remember that they are reading, and that is what counts, when you encounter literary letters that go on for days about buying the perfect pair of skates.

Be sure to provide numerous reference books for your class library. World and U.S. atlases are essential, along with a couple of dictionaries, and any one- or two-volume encyclopedias you can get your hands on. A college catalogue and student handbook are helpful, as well as a thesaurus, a writing handbook, and a state map. *Internet for Dummies* is a new book on my cart, since NKU just entered the 1980s by getting on the 'Net, along with a number of both Mac and DOS beginner books. I also keep books on resume writing, etiquette, and astrological signs, and I tear record reviews out of *RollingStone* magazine. Books on planning a wedding are popular, as well as the safer-sex and birth control brochures students are encouraged to take and keep. With reference books, be creative. There is always a need to know.

Oh, and as my colleagues reminded me to mention, students will not read old books. While they might read *Jurassic Park* and decide to explore Michael Crichton's earlier works like *The Andromeda Strain*, they are not about to touch the copy you bought in 1973. Would you? Do you want to read a book that has brittle, yellowed pages coated with enough dust to make you sneeze your head off? When you shop in used bookstores, as I often do, make sure you buy books that look as if the original owner never got beyond page thirty. And if twelve students beat the hell out of a copy of *The Firm* in a single semester, replace it. And never, but never, bother with books that have had the front cover removed. Forget the ethics of buying these books that sellers have reported damaged or destroyed, but keep in mind that students often choose books based on the cover art alone. These "illegal" books simply do not provide students with the kind of information they need to decide what to read.

Bridge Books

As I have grown more adept at understanding students' interests and gauging their ability, and since I now have a half-dozen colleagues giving me tips from their reading workshops, I am in much better shape to help students explore the kinds of literature that would please even the most discriminate. My mind is pretty much wide open about books, but I understand that novels in which craft is as important as plot put different demands on readers. Books that require reflection, delay gratification, and ask the reader to provide his or her own significance also exercise the mind in new ways. I want to see my students become flexible and undaunted readers, with tastes that alternate, like mine, from the ridiculous to the sublime.

For new readers, the secret to moving them out of their comfort zone is suggesting a book that they will immediately recognize as impressively more demanding than ones they are used to reading, but one you are sure they will be able to manage. To motivate them, present the book, whatever it is, as luridly as possible. Alice Walker's *The Color Purple* can be described as a story about incest, abuse, lesbianism, and revenge. You can hold off on saying that the book is about a nearly broken woman's climb back up to self-respect and spiritual grace until *after* the student commits. I am exaggerating again. Many students would find the second characterization of the Walker novel appealing enough, but my point is that it helps if you can build a bridge between what you know students do like and what they *will* like about the more demanding books you recommend.

There are a number of highly literary works I call "bridge" novels because they help students cross over from easy reads to books that require more work, patience, and reflection. Give me a student who likes to read about Jeffrey Dahmer and what I see is a student who can handle long books filled with detail. I see a student who is interested in questions of evil and illness, as well as whether or not civilization is just about ready to crawl off and die. Students who can whiz through true-crime books are ready and often willing to give more demanding literature about crime and punishment a try. No matter how finely crafted and innovative, Truman Capote's *In Cold Blood* is a true-crime book, when all is said and done. So is Norman Mailer's *The Executioner's Song*. Pat Barker's disturbing novel *Blow Your House Down* is about a working-class woman who makes ends meet through part-time prostitution. When a killer begins ripping apart her friends and neighbors, poor women who engage in the same trade, this woman decides to bait a trap and kill the killer herself. This book is not a thriller. It suggests that if we killed everyone who himself has the potential to kill, the streets would run red. Jane Smiley gained name recognition with *One Thousand Acres*, but she wrote a number of novels before that, and one was *Duplicate Keys*. This book has the most understandable motive for murder I have ever heard or read. I too could kill for these reasons. Rosellen Brown's *Before and After*, finally available in paperback, is pretty tough for my students, but they are pulled into a completely credible "what if?" What if your teenage son, out of nowhere, bludgeoned his girlfriend to death? What would happen to your thoughtfully middle-class life? What would happen to your other child? Would you lie? Tell the truth? Beg for mercy? Or would your own blood turn cold?

Now, as Wanda Crawford pointed out after she read an early draft of this chapter, getting students to read one highly literary book does not automatically mean that they will read—or even be able to identify—another. She is right, as she usually is, but I do devote a number of minilessons to why some books are sold in grocery stores and why others are not. My furtive and probably unrealistic hope is that students who are indeed ready for these books will find them more satisfying and will either seek out others on their own or will respond with a sense of recognition when they are asked to read similarly engaging literary works in the literature classes they are required to take as part of the general studies agenda.

Why They Read

Students have come up with as many reasons for reading as there are reasons to breathe or books to read. In that first class, Kim read a financial management book with the intention of putting her family's affairs in order. Lucy wanted to know more about her heritage and so read ethnic literature. Needing to learn about American dating customs in a hurry, Hiroko blazed through a dozen teen romances. Jerry read to prove something to his old man. Wishing she had been eighteen in 1968 instead of in 1990, Kelly read about the origins of the ultimate hippie band, The Grateful Dead, and then cleaned me out of books about and recordings of Janis Joplin and the Doors to occupy her summer. Anna read because she wanted to understand what her college-educated husband and his friends were talking about. When I start digging into students' letters in Chapters 5 and 6, you will hear these students speak for themselves about why they read what they do. But there have been many other students in my workshops since that first group of eighteen, and by including a few of their reasons for reading, I can give you a better idea of what to expect, as well as a few ideas for a minilesson about why people read.

One of my first observations about workshop was that the books students read in class were not necessarily the books they most enjoyed reading. In that first class, Mac labored his way through "manly" books in class, but outside class consumed the teen romances his female classmates were reading and gushing over. Eventually, he told me this in a literary letter because he was concerned that I would think he was slacking since he had made so little progress with his war books. Like Hiroko, he was looking for dating cues in these teen romances. About a year ago, a student named Mary caught up with me one day before class and asked if we could talk.

"Jeanne, you know how I'm reading those books about emergency room medicine for class? Well, can I write to you about some other books I've been reading?"

"Sure. Whatever you like."

"Thanks. And please don't ask about these other books in the status of the class."

"Okay," I said, wondering why students so often assume I am an insensitive half-wit.

"Here," Mary said and handed me a letter. "This explains."

I did not want to read Mary's letter while she could and

probably would watch me read it, just in case it contained surprises that would register on my transparent face. What I later learned was that she was reading books on recovering from the loss of a child to sudden infant death syndrome. This young and bereft mother had turned to books for help in coping with what can only be the worst possible pain. I was relieved I had not read her letter in the classroom.

Michael had a compelling reason to read, but as I soon figured out, he had little idea where to turn for the information he wanted. First he wrote about an article he had read on gays in the military. He was incensed that some people believed gay and lesbian personnel could not be trusted to share same-sex barracks without compromising their comrades' delicate sensibilities or worse. I wrote back that I agreed. Michael's next letter was about a chapter on homosexuality he had discovered in his psychology textbook. The penny dropped, so I wrote back, "Michael, I know at least a dozen good novels with gay and lesbian characters, if you're not burnt out on the topic. Armistead Maupin's *Tales of the City* is one of the funniest books I've ever read, and so is John Reid's *The Best Little Boy in the World*. I have them at home, so I'll bring them for the cart." Michael read all of Armistead Maupin's *Tales of the City* series, along with Laura Z. Hobson's *Consenting Adult*. He plowed through the late Randy Shilts's *The Band Played On* and *The Mayor of Castro Street*, along with Rita Mae Brown's *Rubyfruit Jungle*. I had to raid the books-for-days gay library of my friend Angus Martin to keep Michael supplied. Eventually, Michael articulated the obvious, and his letters allowed me a view of his journey toward self-awareness.

Reading not only provides singularly elaborated information, it is also the most affordable and available source of lifelong learning, yet it is a useless resource for those who are not inclined to read, not now and not ever. In all honesty, it amazes me that my students have to be led to water before they will drink, when they were clearly thirsty. But there you have it.

What Happened Here?

What I would not do in exchange for a guarantee that these students' reading would last, but all I can say with assurance is that for these shining moments of workshop, we read like we never had before. But why? What happened to make these entrenched nonreaders pick up book after book? It had to be more than opportunity. It had to be more than the external motivation of a grade or dirty looks from the teacher. As I scratched my head over this one, I remembered a chapter called "After the Study: Three Epilogues," in Carole Edelsky's book *Writing in a Bilingual Program: Habia Una Vez* (1986). Edelsky poses a painful premise that there are two kinds of reading and writing, that which is authentic and that which is inauthentic or simulated. She puts simulated "reading" and "writing" in quotation marks to differentiate them from the real thing. The chapter shamed me when I read it in 1987, because I realized that at least three quarters of what I asked students to do in my preworkshop courses was simulated reading and writing, by Edelsky's definition. And what was worse, after reading her article, I knew it in my gut.

As I toiled to write up my dissertation, I talked to Linda Amspaugh, chair of my doctoral committee, about how I thought Edelsky's discussion of authenticity might explain why my students had started reading.

"You don't remember, do you?" Linda said, smiling.

"What?"

"When did you read that Edelsky article?"

"In Karin's class."

"Then you took my class, and all you talked about was authentic reading and writing. You were going crazy trying to find a way to provide students with authentic reading and writing experiences."

"And you handed me *In the Middle*," I said and laughed.

"You got it, Kid. I didn't draw the theoretical conclusion you're seeing, but I saw the pedagogical relationship between authentic reading and workshop."

"Look what you got started."

"I am looking," she said and rifled through the early chapters of the dissertation.

Edelsky has several ideas about what makes reading inauthentic, but the one that got under my skin was what she has to say about purpose. When students read "out of another person's intentions," Edelsky writes, *"without adopting them as their own*, the purpose of compliance interferes with the accomplishment of those other purposes owned by the person who gave the assignment" (174). *Yes.* Surely it has happened to you too. A teacher assigns a book, maybe even a book you would love under other circumstances, and suddenly the reading becomes a chore. I remember having to read *Mrs. Dalloway* in a women's literature class. Woolf was an important writer, a protofeminist, expert at stream of consciousness and depicting the interior landscape. But what a yawn, three hundred pages about a single day in the life of one woman. At age eighteen, I would gladly have led Virginia to the river myself. I bitterly resented my professor, who seemed neither to know nor care that this book put me off, and I read so unwillingly that I mocked and scorned the book. There was no room for me to find my own take on *Mrs. Dalloway*, to search out personal meanings that is, since I was both too hostile to bother and clearly expected to regard the work as Important or else look like the dolt I might very well have been.

Well, I was not damaged by having to read *Mrs. Dalloway* or the dozens of other deadly dull books I was assigned throughout high school and college, but then I was already an avid reader. But what about nonreaders like my students? I suffered through Virginia Woolf and wrote it off as a stupid book. My students suffered through *The Deerslayer* and thought either that they could not read, or that reading was not for them. Their letters reflected frustration and hostility as they discussed other reading or English classes, including mine. Holly had this to say: "I wish in high school you could learn what you liked to read instead of just what they MAKE you read. Then maybe I would have enjoyed reading." Kim wrote, "In school I never could understand anything we read." One student wrote, "Am I supposed to believe that there were no black writers when I went to high school? Why didn't I know about Richard Wright then?" LeeAnn wrote, about someone else's college reading class, "I don't know if you know this, but I took this class last semester and *failed*! I know it was mostly my fault because I just could not get into that class. She is a very nice teacher as a lady, but I did not enjoy her class or reading it her way. It was very boring." Ray's last letter of the semester included this bombshell: "If you had taught the class this way last year I wouldn't have flunked it. What *was* all that junk you wanted us to read?" So much for all our good intentions. They are *our* intentions, after all.

In workshop, compliance means reading books, but other than that, the purposes and pleasures to which students put their reading are entirely their own. I told you about Kim, Lucy, Hiroko, Kelly, Mary, and Michael. Some students read because they thought it would help them in college, others read because they wanted to plan vacations, to scare themselves silly, or to develop strategies for buying good used cars. This was not the simulated reading Edelsky describes, these students read to pursue their own intentions and to make their own meanings. These students were non-"readers," not nonreaders. They had rejected "reading," the simulations Edelsky details, but they took to the real thing, reading, without much fuss.

I think my students, like Bartleby, preferred not, when it came to reading, because they had rejected the reading they encountered in school, and I suspect that they simply had no idea there were other kinds of reading experiences to be had. At home, there were few books and few readers, so where were they going to get acquainted with real reading? One thing that shores up this conclusion for me is the students who get themselves mired in inappropriate novels for weeks on end. They are able to read fewer than ten pages in class each day, clearly never read outside class, and yet they insist the book is "good" when I ask if things are going okay. But their reading is inauthentic. They are complying, rather than reading, because they need to pass the class and will struggle with books that are too slow, too long, or too hard as long as I let them. See, they still do not get it. They have not yet been swept away by a delicious book, so they fail to recognize that reading can be more than the hard labor to which they have consigned themselves. Now, I cut students off after two weeks. I give them time to hit their stride, but if it does not happen, I get them out of the book and work like a fool to help them find novels they can eat alive. If they are to give reading another chance, I am convinced, they have to experience the real thing.

Think about the other kinds of reading we serve up in school. Edelsky argues that most of what we ask students to read, from basal readers to college textbooks, is simulated reading (178). Textbooks fall under Edelsky's definition of inauthentic texts because "one set of pragmatic constraints prevents the operation of another set" (168). We use textbooks because they are comprehensive, ostensibly objective, and never controversial, but those constraints guarantee that the writing is deadly dull. The information textbooks are supposed to transmit was not won without blood, sweat, tears, feuds, and great passion, but the pragmatic constraints of "objective information delivery" overpower any possibility for evocative writing. If textbook reading is how students have come to define reading, is it any wonder that they would rather watch TV?

We also divest literature of its authenticity. Our decidedly "academic" approach to the study of literature entails selecting the great works students will read. Next, we ask students what they think, ignore that, and then tell them what these works are generally accepted by literary scholars to have meant. What we evaluate is whether or not students were able to grasp, apply, and support the lofty interpretations we hand them. This is not authentic reading, by Edelsky's definition, because "meaning creation" is not central to the process (168), it is secondary to the goal of instilling in students an awareness of the rigorous textual analyses of professionals. Again, back to my own schooling for an example. In high school, I was expected to read the Flannery O'Connor short story, "Everything That Rises Must Converge" and to understand it as a study of Southern whites' resentment of the emergence of the black middle class, as symbolized by the identical hats worn by both the white and black matrons who figure prominently in the story. At least that was what my high school English teacher said the story meant, and I remember being terrifically impressed by her depth. Like me, many young readers would have to be led by the nose to this sophisticated analysis of race and class before they could report or support it, but that was what lectures were for.

When I wrote my paper on "Everything That Rises Must Converge," I sounded like I knew what I was talking about as I parroted my teacher's analysis, but I could no more have produced that interpretation than I could have legally purchased beer at the convenience store down the street from the school. What the story had meant to me was that it reminded me of a rotten day in sixth grade when a girl we called "K-Mart Kim" came to school wearing the same outfit I was. The beating I took from my social-climbing classmates shamed me into never wearing the clothes again. Reading Flannery O'Connor's story made me feel the pettiness I should have felt then. I rewrote the teacher's impressive interpretation for my class assignment, but the second short story I ever wrote (and never showed my English teacher) was about the bitchery and insecurity K-Mart Kim's clothes had brought out in me as an eleven-year-old. The teacher provided me with a sophisticated, eye-opening, and public (i.e., shared) interpretation of the story. But the meaning I made, while highly significant to me, was unlikely to be shared by other readers. My unique and limited experience obviously shaped the meaning I made. Yet I learned as much from my personal understanding of the story as I did from my teacher's interpretation. Sometimes our students, and most definitely we ourselves, prefer the sound of our own schooled and expert voices, but personal meanings are at least part of what inspires us to stare at small print for hours at a time.

Listen, I seem to be saying that the reading they do in school is what put these students off the whole idea of picking up books. But it gets worse. Something else I learned from studying that first class was that their workshop reading was largely untroubled. As you will see in Chapter 5, they were able to summarize effectively the books they read and to offer interpretations and then support them. They thought about what they read, and they monitored what they considered improvements in their ability. They noted what was difficult and often solved their own problems, such as how to approach an unfamiliar dialect or what environmental conditions would be more conducive to their reading. They knew when they had not understood, and they knew when they were not likely to *be* understood. In their definitive review of strategic reading, Paris, Wasik, and Turner identify several strategies associated with sound reading; these include reflection, metacognition, perceptions of competence and control, and the ability to summarize (1991, 610–21). What? My remedial students were behaving just like strategic readers?

Wait a minute. Remember their Nelson-Denny scores? These eighteen students were, on average, five years below grade level in reading, this was no honor's class, so how come they were doing what good readers do? Edelsky's theory of authenticity once again comes to the rescue. Not only is most of the reading done in school simulated, says Edelsky, we evaluate students' ability based on instruments, like the Nelson-Denny, that measure their proficiency with simulated reading (176). In theory, at any rate, these instruments give us an understanding of our students as "readers" but, as in this case, how they handled themselves as readers came as something of a surprise. These students read just fine, even though they embarrassed themselves when it came to "reading." My conclusion is that all readers are good readers, when they have the right book. But this does not mean much when the chalkmarks of accomplishment are measured solely in terms of simulated reading.

🌿 *Chapter 5*

Literary Letters

*T*here is very little reason for us to write letters any more. AT&T has wired up the world, so I can forget what time it is and call and wake up my mother just as easily from New Zealand as I can from Northern Kentucky. And all you have to do is "surf the 'Net," as my students say, to know that you can e-mail a friend a thousand miles away faster than you can lick a stamp and walk to the post office. And fax machines! I love these things. Words out of wires. But even though we have little reason to write letters anymore, we still do. I suspect we always will. Letters get things on record, and we seem to like that. People can also say things in letters they are unwilling to say face-to-face, like "I am leaving you" or "I think I love you" or "It has come to our attention." We like that about letters too. There are letters of application, intent, thanks, apology, invitation, regret, condolence, recommendation, and acceptance. And what about chain letters? The part of your brain that evolved over the last ten million years knows these things need to be promptly transported to the trash, but your more primitive, reptilian tissue makes you hesitate, wondering what the vengeful gods will send your way if you break the chain. The mere sight of certain letters in the box can instantly take your blood pressure up a notch, but then there is nothing like getting your hands on a letter you have been longing to see. Letters get to us.

It was inevitable that letter writing would find its way into the classroom. For years we have been asking students to write letters to the editor or to the president or to soldiers stationed overseas. Sometimes these exchanges are merely one-sided exercises in audience, but I once asked my Northern students to write to the college students I was teaching in a maximum security prison for youthful offenders. A lesson in audience awareness was had by all. One of my freshmen asked an incarcerated student if he was looking forward to going home for Christmas, and one of the prison students asked why all college kids drove Corvettes. I wanted the exchange to continue, as did both sets of students, but the prison administrators went ape and I had to abandon the plan. We get to know each other well through letters, sometimes too well.

Asking students to address those letters to us, their teachers, and for us then to write back a reply, does not seem to have occurred to anyone until the mid-sixties, when a sixth-grade teacher named Leslee Reed engaged her students in on-going letter exchanges about their lives and academic work that came to be known as dialogue journals (Staton et al. 1988). And of course, Nancie Atwell (1984, 1987) later developed "literary letters," in which the student-teacher letter exchange focused entirely on reading. But I had some questions about these literary letters. In Nancie Atwell's skilled hands, the letters were collaborative, involved and involving, mutual. But not everyone is the teacher Nancie Atwell is. I had seen response journals, a format intended to give students an opportunity to explore meaning, corrupted by colleagues. One in particular told me she used journals as a means of "letting students get their silly ideas out of their systems before I tell them what the piece is about." So what would the letters be like in my novice hands? I wondered about the extent to which these letters could be collaborative, given the unequal authority and expertise of the correspondents. While *collaboration* can be defined as joint intellectual endeavor, it is also the word used to describe treasonable cooperation. Would I use letters to do what reading teachers traditionally seem to fall back on—telling students the meaning of what they have just read—or would I help sustain, maintain, and extend their reading? Bottom line, I studied literary letters because I was dying to know what students might write in them, as well as whatever I might say in response.

The Letters, First Glance

Like all correspondents, the students and I got to know each other better through the course of these letter exchanges. Although we stuck to the topic of books and reading like a pair of new sneakers to hot summer tar, we revealed ourselves through the kinds of remarks we habitually made. We shared philosophies of life, political points of view, and personal experiences. The students understood that these letters were not personal correspondence but a very particular kind of correspondence about books. I get students off to the right start by, once again, plundering something from Nancie Atwell's *In the Middle* (1987) and rewriting it in my own style. I take a description of literary letters Ms. Atwell wrote for her students (193) and write a personally addressed form letter to each of my students about what we might want to talk about in these letters. The text reads:

Dear

This is my first literary letter to you. You read about them in the syllabus, and you heard me mention them in class, but I think I still have a lot of explaining to do about these letters. Literary letters are a place for you, me, and your classmates to talk about books, reading, authors, and writing. You'll discuss the books you read in letters to me and your classmates, and we'll write back to you.

In your letters talk with us about what you've read. Tell what the books made you think and feel. Were you irritated about a character's stupid choices, like going into a dark room no one in his or her right mind would go into when there is a voice in the house whispering "get out"? You know just what I mean, don't you? Did you love the happy ending or think it was a crock? Was the movie better or worse?

Tell what these books said and meant to you. Do you worry about the state of the world when you read about sicko stuff? Do you think there is such a thing as true love? Are people either good or bad, or is there a lot of room for confusion between the two?

If you want to know what we think, you have only to ask. Ask me what I think of the death penalty. Ask a classmate what to do if you can't find enough time to read. Tell us if a book is boring you out of your mind, and ask us what you might want to read next.

We'll write back with questions of our own, along with ideas, and our own humble opinions. Don't be shy. Tell us what you think of what we have to say, as well as what we're reading. Tell us about books we won't want to miss. And if the dog don't bark, tell us what books to avoid.

Talk it up!

Best,
Jeanne

In all, these eighteen students wrote two hundred and twelve literary letters to me. Each student was required to write twelve letters to me and twelve to a classmate to receive an A for that portion of his or her final grade. On average, each student wrote twelve letters to me, but the actual range of letters written in that first class was from a low of nine to a high of seventeen. While I urged students to write at least a page, single-spaced, the average length of these letters was two pages, or three hundred and fifty to four hundred words. I wrote a total of two hundred and eight letters in response to these eighteen students. My letters averaged a page in length, or about two hundred words, with a range of one to four pages when I really got going. While I did not analyze the letters students wrote to each other (but look for the sequel), I did count student-to-student letters and, on average, each student wrote fifteen letters to classmates. I include the counts and averages to stress that we wrote a lot during reading workshop, much more than I had ever before asked of students in a reading class.

One of the first things I learned about the letters was that students have clear notions of correspondence in their heads, and they pattern their letters just like any other letters they might write, using salutations and closings, along with a postscript or two. There is some pitching and slanting until they get comfortable with how to address me, though. For example, a nontraditional student who was very concerned about doing everything by the book consulted *The Little Brown Handbook*, and her first letter to me followed the business letter guidelines of that reference. I wrote back, "Dear Ms. Vivian, Having received your correspondence of January 17, I am writing to encourage you to relax." Vivian's next letter began: "Hey, you." Most students are comfortable addressing me by my first name, as in "Dear Jeanne." Dave, who you will read quite a lot about, never began a letter with anything other than "Yo, Teach."

I always address students as "Dear" in letters, and close with "Thanks for writing." The students end their letters with a variety of closings, such as: "Your friend, Holly," "Your student, Lance," "Yours in Jesus, Ray" (a joke regarding our shared status as non-Christians), or "XXOO, Dave." But in that first workshop, several students ended with the letters "WBS" printed after their names. I could not pin the tail on that donkey. I had no idea what "WBS" meant. I was reluctant to ask, knowing that my total lack of cool would be on display for the entire class, but I steeled myself up with the reminder that I was doing educational research here and had to rise above a concern for my image. I dragged Sara aside one day and asked the meaning of this mysterious code.

"WBS? It means *write back soon*." Sara could barely contain the roller-coaster roll of her eyes. "Jeanne, if somebody wrote SWAK, would you know what that meant?"

"Yes, of course," I said, lying through my teeth. *Write back soon*. I think they meant it.

Students also use postscripts in their letters. Most of the time, these postscripts convey personal information, which is out of bounds in the body of the letters. Dave wrote, "I bought that car I told you about. It looks like a sack of shit but it runs good. Me and Dad spent the weekend with the owners manual and replaced every part that was under $10." Anna penned, "My husband's friends talked about a Newsweek article on Saturday. I told them I preferred inspirational works such as Dr. Norman Vincent Peale." Kelly wrote, "I just heard the Cowboy Junkies for the first time. Excuse me. But you like this band? Tell me what I'm missing." I use postscripts in the same way, asking about a bad cold (which becomes very apparent in an otherwise silent classroom), weekend plans, or what students called "Kevorkian classes." There are times when the postscripts are longer than the letters, but I like it that we have a place to shoot the breeze.

Another aspect of real-world correspondence students bring to their letters is etiquette. Owing someone a letter, including the teacher, is lowdown and rude. Students think either they are being snubbed or the person they have written to is an unorganized mess. One day in that first class, Valerie cornered Jerry and said, "If you don't write me back pretty soon I'm gonna think you don't love me." Jerry responded, "You write better than me and read books I can't understand. It's not personal." When I had not heard from Mac for two weeks, I wrote him another letter and got my reply before the end of class, "Thanks for the letter. I'm sorry I didn't answer the one before that. I should tell you what's taking so long with this book." Ray wrote regularly to me, but he signed, sealed, and delivered very few to his classmates. One morning he turned his folder upside down and, when nothing fell out, he announced, "I didn't get a single letter."

Hiroko, who almost never spoke up in class said, "And when you don't write what did you expect?"

"I wrote you twice, man," Dave added, "so where's my special delivery?"

Lucy added, "Trifling with me about no mail. Here is a pen and here is some paper, mister."

Ray arrived at class the next meeting with enough xeroxed copies of an apologetic form letter to distribute to the entire class. After that, he kept up with his correspondence.

Of course I wanted to know if these letters sustained both reading and reflection. They did both. But there was no cognitive razzle-dazzle at work here, no breakthrough methodological brilliance. These students wrote because of good old Emily Post. Owing a person a letter gets up close and personal when you see him or her three times a week. While students can "owe" a teacher a paper without feeling any social discomfort, these letters are different. It *is* personal. To "owe" a letter to the teacher or to a classmate is to ignore the personal interest someone took in you. In my workshop classes, in most cases, this is just not done. And in order to write letters, students had to have something to write about, which meant that they had to be reading. A student who was not reading had nothing to discuss, except why he or she was not reading, and that wore thin quicker than the seat of a Rollerblader's shorts. If students were to participate in letter writing, and they had to since they were regularly getting mail, they had to read. It was as simple as that.

There are also some ugly elements of real-world correspondence that can creep into the literary-letter exchange. This has not happened in any of my classes, but I should have seen it coming. My colleague Patty Fairbanks recently told me that a male student in her class had been using his literary letters to hit on a female classmate. The woman complained to Patty, since the advances were unwelcome and inappropriate, and Patty reminded her students that they were to use their letters to discuss reading. In my classes, students' letters are public documents. They are kept in folders on the book cart, where anyone has access to them, and the students know that I read through them. Honest, it is research, not nosiness, but that may be why I have avoided what, in hindsight, seems like an obvious potential misuse. Another possibility I now see, and one to nip in the bud, is proselytizing. Our campus is plagued by some very pushy fundamentalist groups that target freshmen.

Another potential problem with literary letters, and one I have encountered, is that you may get a student like Paulie, a sweet but strange young man. I risk revealing his identity if I explain too much, but the boy's behavior was oddly ritualistic and repetitive, and his classmates were put off. Paulie wrote to everyone, and no one wrote back, except me, of course, and he was terribly hurt by the rejection. I lost sleep and wrote to him three times a week, before I finally took two older male students aside, one at a time, and asked for their help. I told them that Paulie's letters were really interesting and that he could use a pen pal in the worst way. These two compassionate men corresponded with Paulie for the rest of the semester. At the end of the class, Hank thanked me for hooking him up with Paulie by saying, "He has a way of looking at things that makes a lot of sense, just turned inside out."

And do not be surprised if you get an Erika or two in class. What we have here is a very bright student with a chip on her shoulder big enough to level Hong Kong. Why is this kid in your class? Who knows. Perhaps she does not test well, or has been labeled ADD or dyslexic or otherwise learning disabled. The short and skinny is that she is among the walking wounded, as defensive as a hooded cobra, and about as likable. Grab your antivenin and ask for the patience of a saint, because you are in for a wild ride. Witness this:

Erika to Anna, "You actually like that sack of shit Danielle Steel?"

Erika, during status of the class, "Oh so, big brainer, you finished another Sweet Valley High book? My dog read that last week."

Erika to Dave, "You ought to be in rehab, you know. Oh, I forgot. You already are."

Such a mouth. The Erikas of the world need total attention, approval, and sincere praise, but they also need a talking to.

When Erika told a classmate, "Any guy who reads about his football hero is a closet fag just like everybody in the NFL," I nabbed her after class.

"Erika, I want you to stop putting down your classmates and what they read. The point is that they're reading. They're not where you're at, but you don't need to dump on them."

"So I'm supposed to be nice?"

"No, no, no. I want you to be more than nice. I want you to be a cheerleader for literacy."

"Do I really read better than them?"

"Honestly, I don't know. But you read more challenging books. You have a lot of insight about what you read too."

"Except I read like I'm nine."

"That's what this is all about, isn't it?"

I had to hide my shock when her eyes filled up. "It sucks you know." Her face was very red as she tried not to cry. "Too dumb to be smart and too smart to be dumb. So, okay," she said and headed for the door. "I'll try not to be a bitch."

"Erika."

She stopped but still would not look at me. "It's all right to be a bitch about LaVyrle Spencer."

The kid turned and slammed me with a high five so hard my hand stung. "Don't I know it," she said and was gone.

Erika only slipped once after that, but she was sitting next to me and for once she did not intend for everyone in the room to hear. I know you have taught Erikas before, but watch out for them in workshop, since literary letters give them so much opportunity to do damage. Talk to them, try to be understanding and, if that fails, remember to hide the body.

A Two-Way Street

One thing I really wanted to know about these letters was whether or not they were interactive. After several months of nosing about in the letters, I came to the depressing conclusion that interaction was a one-way street. I answered nearly every question a student asked me, but they answered only about a third of the follow-up questions I asked them. I could picture Lloyd Benson of Texas saying, "You, m'am, are no Nancie Atwell." In her hands, the letters were interactive. In mine, literary letters were simply the same bored book reports and teacher follow-up comments. I was wailing away about this to Chet Laine, one of my dissertation committee members, and he said, "Have you looked at anything other than the question/answer ratio as evidence of interaction?" Oh.

I pulled out all four hundred and twenty letters and read them again, and then it began to hit me. The students and I acted upon each other in a dozen different ways. The students were not writing to me as some abstraction called "audience" or "teacher," they were writing to *me*. They wanted to make sure *I* understood what they had to say. Look at the number of times they backtracked to explain important details they had left out. Holly's first novel was a horror story called *The Mirror*. After explaining that an "evil" mirror had caused a grandmother, Brandy, and her granddaughter, Shay, to switch bodies and time periods, Holly wrote, "And she [Brandy] really don't know how to react to the fact that Shay's got a baby on the way and she prays every night. Oops. I forgot to tell you that Shay was pregnant before the mirror did the switch and so now Brandy is." As I read and reread the letters, I also realized that students were merciful about explaining unfamiliar jargon or insider terms they picked up from their books. Sara read *Kaffir Boy* and explained that "calling a black in South Africa kaffir is like calling a black in America a n_____. You say kaffir like you would laugher."

I coded the letters by circling potentially significant passages in red and then putting a tiny sticky note bearing the category name on that passage. I had thousands of notes plastered to these letters, so imagine my horror when I arrived home one afternoon to find my cat, Bea, covered in sticky notes after she had had a roll in my data. Sitting on the stairs, very near tears, I pulled a Post-It off her ear and read the category, "student perception of teacher likes/dislike." Huh? It was a category I had not paid much attention to, since I did not know what to make of it, but I immediately saw this as possible evidence of interaction. Neurotic doctoral student that I was, you know I had a backup system, and I had my coding reconstructed in record time. What I learned was that students, like Lance, had picked up quite a lot of information about me and made reference to it in their letters. Lance always provided colorful details about his book *The Frontiersman*, and we often discussed the harshness of pioneer life. He wrote, "I know you said you wouldn't want to live back then (I would!) but you like the outdoors so much, maybe it wouldn't be as terrible as you think." Kelly, my cosmic pal, wrote, "I bet you would've been a Deadhead if you hadn't gone to college. Right?"

Interaction means to act upon one another, and once I got that into my head, I started seeing evidence of it everywhere. After just a few letter exchanges, students are able to predict the kinds of questions I will ask. This may also mean that my questions are predictably teacherly, but who asked you? After reading three teen romances in quick succession, Hiroko, a pre–psychology major fluent in three languages and already able to toss around names like Freud and Jung, wrote, "Why am I reading these books about girls and crushes? I need to know American dating and girl's hopes and dreams. Also I want a romance!" Gary, a recent student, read my mind when he wrote to ask if I had been wondering why a guy like him was reading Armistead Maupin's *Tales of the City*. He explained that his brother was gay and had gotten him to watch the miniseries on PBS, so he wanted to read the book. Gary, who brought a cup to class in which to spit tobacco juice and was enthusiastic about monster truck competitions, read all six of Maupin's San Francisco chronicles.

Once I had revised my view of interaction, I saw that my students worked hard not to spoil my reading by giving away the endings of the books they read and wrote about, in case I wanted to read them. And what is more, they wished to "act upon me" by encouraging me to read their books. Holly wrote, "I could tell you what happened at the end of The Mirror, but then you wouldn't read it. So, you'll just have to wait and see." Jerry, full of himself by the end of the semester, discussed a book called *Twice Pardoned* : "So just like you thought Harold turned out to be a real phony he goes into all this stuff about how finding Jesus was a scam and he goes back to jail for armed robbery. Had you going. That's not what happened. I really think you should read this book." In the spring of 1994, there was a massive campaign, perhaps even a conspiracy, among my students to get me to read *The Bridges of Madison County*. Students came at it from all angles, such as how I would relate to this love story because the characters were "older" (like me, I presume) or because the language was so "poetic" or because they wanted my opinion of the moral dilemma the characters faced.

Several students and I had running jokes, and I think these too indicated that the letters were mutual exchanges. With Jerry, the joke was about my weak stomach, which we started early in the semester. I was eating lunch in my office one day, reading and responding to literary letters, when Jerry stopped by. He asked if I had gotten to his letter yet. I said I had not, and he laughed and enigmatically said, "Enjoy your lunch." When I got to his letter, I knew why. He had been reading a book called *Man Is the Prey*, about different animals feeding upon humans, and had written: "Sharks have been known to bite people in half. They have several rows of teeth that are as sharp as razor blades." I ended my letter back with the comment "Thanks for ruining my lunch." Afterward, Jerry took every opportunity to include gruesome details in his letters. This was a typical Jerry gem: "Hyenas usually live off dead meat but they sometimes track a smell of blood and kill that animal. A lot of times natives are killed in their huts when the hyenas think they are dead and try to eat them and sometimes eat them anyway." We joked about the amount of weight I was losing by reading his letters at lunch, and I began to write questions asking for ever more disgusting details. For Ray and me, the running joke in our letters was our shared aversion to Christian fundamentalism. In response to Jason Miller's *That Championship Season*, Ray wrote: "I have never seen the Lord's name taken in vain so many times. I'd wash this writer's mouth out with soap if I had my way. I think we ought to put this on our to-burn list, Sister Jeanne."

I have tried just about every writing-about-reading activity known to the profession. Formal explications are no good for beginners because they do not offer any wiggle room. The writer is supposed to at least *sound* sure of what he or she is saying about a book. Note taking and summary writing are pointless exercises if a student already understands the material and useless if he or she does not. I mean how does trying to summarize a passage help you understand it if you do not? No amount of close reading or rereading will help the uncomprehending to comprehend. Short essay responses make the teacher (or the textbook author) the one who determines what is worth discussion. And response journals, although they allow students to explore meaning in a freewheeling way, get pretty murky in terms of audience. Who are students writing these journals for? The teacher? Posterity? Literary letters are most like response journals, because they allow students to explore the meanings they find important, but we are still talking hemispheres away in terms of differences.

The audience in literary letters is not at all ambiguous. My students asked about my sick dog. They knew exactly how to arouse my curiosity about a book. They explained themselves and asked if I had understood. They displayed a sensitivity to readerly needs and an awareness of audience that novice writers just are not supposed to have. Who knew they could do that? These "poor" readers were able to retell their books with great clarity and personal style. I am convinced the issue of ambiguity matters, too. In a 1988 study involving response journals, Marilyn Sternglass, a pioneer among those who are looking at the reciprocal nature of the reading and writing processes, found that "the absence of a real audience from a writer's perspective has the potential to decrease substantially the commitment a writer puts into a piece of writing" (144). I can second that. As a doctoral student asked to keep about three-dozen response journals, so that journaling might be modeled for me, I never knew for whom I was writing. Could I say an article I had been asked to read was bullshit? Could I say that only if I supported it? Could I say *bullshit* at all? Were my professors reading to see if I understood? if we agreed? Were they even reading these things at all?

Listen, there can be a lot of ambiguity for us in responding to journals as well. When we write back, in end comments or marginalia, do we expect our questions to be answered, or are we just providing food for thought? How do we know whether students even read our comments? They certainly doubt us. I know I have come across comments like "Are you really reading this?" buried in journal entries. What a righteous feeling to be able to scribble back, yes, this time. These students read my letters, and I read theirs. There is no way we could doubt one another. Literary letters may raise other limitations of audience, in that there are still things I would not say to a student, such as "I think you're a frightening right-wing freak to endorse such a book." And there are topics they will not raise with me, such as the sexual content of their books, even when they know that I know they are reading very sexy books. But we have to draw the line somewhere.

Summary Writing

I was a mess during that first workshop class. I did not have a lot of time to reflect on the letter exchange, since I was up to my elbows in literary letters, research, graduate course work, and the two other classes I taught, but I knew from the very beginning that the students' letters were filled with plot summary. I kept a teaching journal throughout my research, and my comments indicate I had myself in an uproar:

"They're writing too much summary." "What am I going to do about all this summary?" "If I suggest they write less summary, will they just write shorter letters?" My assumption was that summary writing, especially in response to literature, was uncritical, unselective, lazy, low-down, and dumb. In learning hierarchies, the rank of summary writing is roughly equivalent to that of where coelenterates fall in the food chain. If literary letters produced so much summary, as least in my instructional hands, I had to wonder how valuable they really could be.

Once again, professor Chet Laine, patron of strung out doctoral students, listened to me talk this through. All he said was, "Now you hadn't read most of the books the students did, right?" Right. So? Oh. These students read ninety-three different books, only fifteen of which I had read previously, and many of those I had read ten or more years ago. When any two people discuss a book one of them has not read, there is an obvious need for a little summation of the plot. I was so used to artificial talk with my students about reading, I did not recognize the real thing when it was under my nose. Of course they had to summarize the plot if I was going to understand their interpretations of or reactions to their books. I never told students to include enough summary so that I could get a solid sense of what their books were about. They intuitively knew that I would not understand what they had to say about the meaning of a book if I did not know the plot in some detail.

This hunch that students were summarizing for the benefit of their reader rather than because of some character flaw was refined when I broke down students' summary passages into two types: summaries written about books I had read and those produced about books with which I was unfamiliar. All combined, students wrote roughly forty-three thousand words of summary. Eighty-four percent of those many, many words were devoted to summarizing the books I had not read. Only sixteen percent (about seven thousand words) covered those books I had read sometime in the last decade. The students knew that it was not necessary to summarize a book that I had already read, unless they needed to let me know where they were in the book or to frame an interpretive remark. They wrote *purposeful* summaries, and this was essential if we were to talk coherently about their books.

But I did not let myself or workshop off the hook so easily. Even though these were purposeful summaries, I still wondered if the fact that students needed to devote so much of their writing simply to filling me in might be robbing them of time and attention better spent analyzing their books in more critical or at least more entertaining ways. Was this a problem with workshop? If the teacher has not read the student's book—and even with my regimen of trying to read everything students drag in, I am still unfamiliar with fifty percent of what they read—did the approach foster more summary writing than we might desire? When I raised that question, I was still operating under the belief that writing summaries required little critical thinking. But when I cruised through my students' summary passages again for the third or fourth time, my English teacher assumptions about summary writing started to fall apart.

First, these summaries were not uncritical or unselective. The students boiled down the plots of two- and three-hundred-page books to three to five pages (when totaled—summaries were always interrupted by interpretive comments and written across the course of two to four letters). I have no idea how students decided what to include in their summaries, but clearly each writer made choices about what I needed to know in order not only to understand the book but also to *experience* its dramatic moments. The students also seemed to want to make their summaries compelling, which they did by including important bits of dialogue and vivid descriptive details. Take a look at Jerry's letter about a book called *Twice Pardoned*, Harold Morris's confessional account of his murder conviction and later conversion to Christianity. The climax of the book comes with Morris' arrest, which he had not been expecting:

... a bunch of police officers kicked open the door about 11pm at night. Harold was then put under arrest. He was asked a lot of questions in the police car but he did not answer because he knew his rights.

His bail was set at $10,000. He was in his cell when a FBI agent came in and said that "bail has been dropped for you Harold Morris. You are charged for six armed robberies, and murder one, no bond."

Harold thought this was a nightmare but the bars reminded him that it wasn't.

Lucy's writing was equally vivid. In her summary of an Alice Walker story entitled "Nineteen Fifty-Five," Lucy explained that a character named Traynor, a white singer who became known as the "emperor of rock and roll," had bought all of the songs he sang from a black songwriter who had not been able to break into the music business. Lucy summarized an important moment of the story:

Traynor came by one day to see how Gracie Mae (oh by the way that was her name) was doing and he invited her out to his house for dinner. He had her picked up in a limo and she was speechless when she visited his house. She said he was starting to gain weight and [that he] complained about life a lot. He asked her about the song she wrote. "What did it mean?" She said "you've been singing this song and making a lot of money off this song and do not know what it means?" He did not know what to say.

A passage from one of Lance's letters (putting me in mind of a young Yukio Mishima) also makes my point:

The Shawnee Indian tribe had captured a colonel by the name of Crawford. The torture they put him through was tremendous. They tied him up at the stake, built a fire around him, and beat him. They cut his ears off, stabbed him with hot spears, threw hot coals at him, and at one time while he was still alive his feet were black and began to actually burn. And when they were done playing with him they threw him in the fire.

Because of these detailed and proficient summaries, I had a very clear sense of what students were reading, which helped me understand and respond to their interpretations, hard spots, and enthusiasms. As I wrote to Jerry, "I feel like I'm reading over your shoulder." The students' summaries were detailed enough, their sense of what a reader would need to know precise enough, that most of the plot synopses I provide here are based solely on the knowledge I acquired through the students' writing. Now, it is not as if I were the only one who considered summary writing as a shallow way for adults to respond to literature. Why is this? In traditional reading and literature classrooms, the teacher has already read the book the student is writing about because, well, he or she assigned it. We do not need to be told what we already know, so summary looks like a substitute for substance.

But summary writing proved more than a necessary evil in these literary letters. Because they were purposeful summaries, written for a real audience with a real need to know, students had to write with a sound sense of audience awareness, and they explained themselves, defined their terms, and made their summaries riveting. It is hard enough for any writer to "dissociate from the text and read it through the eyes of potential readers" (Rosenblatt 1989, 167), and this is particularly true for the inexperienced. These students had to imagine what I could reasonably be expected to know about their books, what I might want or need to know, and eventually even the questions I would be likely to ask. This is not a talent that leaps to mind when I think about the writing ability of underprepared freshmen. Even if all students are doing is retelling plot, they are still reflecting on what they have read. As Paris, Wasik, and Turner inform us, good readers "ask questions . . . and invoke strategies to review the text and their comprehension" (1991, 614). In other words, they continue processing after the reading is completed. Now, the act of writing does not guarantee advanced processing, but to summarize a book does require that students review and reconsider its events. The book is reopened, in a sense, after the student is done reading. Students also had to tell me what was happening in the story to support, frame, or explain their thoughts about a character's motivation or psychological make-up or morality. The National Assessment of Educational Progress found that the majority of seventeen-year-olds were not able to provide adequate evidence to support their interpretations (1981, 16–17). Yet my remedial readers were very able to tell me enough about the books they read to explain why they thought the things they did. Go figure.

You bet, literary letters used in a free-choice reading class require students to write considerable summary. But there may be advantages to this situation in which a teacher has not read the book a student is reporting on, regardless of how much summary writing this kind of correspondence demands. And chief among them is the authenticity of the exchange. Carole Edelsky describes one type of inauthentic writing (or "writing," as she abbreviates) as making use of print for the professed purpose of informing an audience that, in reality, is better informed than the writer (1986, 174). There was no pretense here; I actually was less informed than the students. Yes, I asked them to write these letters—the students may not have had a yearning deep in their souls to talk to me or anyone else about books—but once the exchange was set in motion, it was authentic. The students accepted "the ostensible purpose," telling me about their books, "as their own" (Edelsky 1986, 177). These letters, with their jokes and confidences, their engagement, and their efforts to explain, insist on the authenticity of the exchange.

Interpreting

When you come from a background in literature, your plan is to teach students to better *interpret* what they read. *To interpret is to explain.* But in the field of college reading, our goal is to teach students to better comprehend what they read. *To comprehend is to understand.* To explain a book is to make something out of it—meaning. To understand a book is to take in meaning. And there you have the down-and-dirty difference between literary and traditional reading theories. Literary theory regards the reader as more active, someone who makes meaning of text and then accounts for it. Traditional reading theory, and by that I mean data-driven and interactive models, see the role of the reader as more passive, since meaning is regarded as in the text itself, to be extracted rather than constructed. I know you have heard all this before, but I want to be clear that I do not use the words *comprehend* and *interpret* interchangeably. I know my students comprehended what they read. They clearly understood their books at a literal level. If not, they would have chucked the book. But I was interested in if and how they interpreted what they read. Did they offer explanations of what they read that went beyond an understanding of who did what to whom?

When I think back, so much of what my students wrote that I understood as interpretation would be considered digressions, maybe even daydreams, from the point of view of traditional reading theory. Their thoughts about what they read, as well as how they arrived at these meanings, would be irrelevant on a comprehension test, to most short-answer questions found in textbooks, and in some teachers' minds. When Sara read *Kaffir Boy*, she devoted pages and pages of her letters to a comparison of white rule in South Africa to slavery in America. This topic was not an issue in the book, but it seized Sara's attention and made her think for herself. She went after the complex issues of race and justice, and her efforts would have been wasted on a comprehension test about the book and had jack to do with the old reading teacher standby: What was the author trying to say? Sara wrote:

> I think Apartheid is worse than slavery in America. With slavery the blacks knew they had no freedom because they were like cows or tractors. The master owned them. But in Apartheid they say that blacks are free just inferior. But when your goverment says you are inferior you are not free because you have to be told what to do because you don't know what's good for you. What do you call that? A mixed message? I think its easier to live with the facts than to have to figure out what's a lie about you.

Sara not only learned about apartheid from her reading, the girl was cooking with fire because of what *she* brought to the book.

When it came to my students' interpretations, no one could really say they had a live-and-let-live attitude. By and large, they were as judgmental as only the very young can be, having had too few years to well and truly screw things up. When reading *The Color Purple*, Lucy's judgment of Celie's stepfather was swift and sure: "He treat her like a dog." After reading the Alice Walker short story, "How Did I Get Away with Killing One of the Biggest Lawyers in the State?" Vivian wrote: "Someone who would let someone, a man of all people, come before their relationship with their family is crazy." By the time he had finished *The Valacchi Papers*, Jerry had concluded that Joseph Valacchi was a "hypocrite." He explained:

> He seemed like he bullshitted about a lot of things in the book. Like he always said, well I have to much respect. In several situation he said that response. What I'm getting at is if he had so much respect about people, then how could he shoot someone, deal drugs to kids, and steal people's hard earn money?

Four students read *Go Ask Alice*, which is purported to be the actual journal of a teenage girl whose involvement in drugs led to her death. LeeAnn made Pat Robertson look like a pussycat when she wrote, "She is disgusting. She has done almost every drug she's capable of doing. She's had sex with numerous men, just for more drugs of course. What a waste. So she died. What did she expect?"

My students have watched enough *Oprah* to have become expert armchair analysts and can explain the behavior of just about any character. About *The Color Purple*, Lucy wrote, "Celie did not have the love that she wanted and needed from her father. That lowered her self-esteem and she did not have pride in herself, she did not think she was worthy of better things. Shug and her sister Nettie gave her that push she needed and that self-worth." When reading a book called *Goodbye Forever*, Joanie explained that the main character, a teenager named Kari, "is afraid to let anyone get close to her probably because her father died when she was young." After finishing the book, Joanie wrote, "Kari's whole attitude toward being afraid to loose a loved one changed. She realized that she would have to face up to this type of thing. She couldn't worry about these things because they might not happen." Valerie, who read and got me to read V. C. Andrews's *Heaven*, seemed fascinated by Heaven's deadbeat father, Luke. "Heaven found out her real mother died after she had her and her pa was never the same. He blamed Heaven for her death and could not stand the resemblance of her to her mother. It is a shame that he is such a drunk and so hung up on his past that he's messing up his future." Students who want to dig deep, who like to explore meaning, will make use of whatever knowledge is at hand to make sense of what they read.

These students, many on the verge of adulthood, others already well-seasoned travelers, gave a lot of thought to how one ought to go about living, and they tested or forged their philosophies of life against what they read. Wary and assertive, Kim insisted that people should "take control before they get taken." Trippy and hip, Kelly's answer to almost everything was "whatever." Kelly's book, *The Official Book of the Dead*, described the lifestyle of Deadheads, fans who followed the Grateful Dead on tour across the country. She wrote, "People don't understand them. They think there pissing their lives off following this band around still being hippies. But if your not hurting anyone what's wrong with doing your own thing? They don't want to be doctors or lawyers. Who needs more lawyers anyway? People shouldn't live being afraid to be different." Lucy's design for living, or philosophy of life, took my breath away. It was Langston Hughes's poem, "Harlem" that finally gave Lucy the refrain—"what happens to a dream deferred"— she needed to clarify her thoughts on life. She wrote:

Many people have dreams. When you're a child you dream about being a doctor, actor, lawyer, business woman or man, president.

And then you think about what it takes to make this dream come true.

Some people get discourage and they feel, "I can't, I'm not smart enough." In that way they shut out their dreams.

Some people are in the process of reaching their dream and then they have a setback of some sort and they feel they will never recover.

For some people a dream can become a reality and for others it can't. It depends on your dream and how bad you want your dream. People who are afraid to dream, or afraid to reach for their dreams are sorry.

I'm going to college and I'm doing some dreaming for my people.

My students reminded me that even an escapist novel can take you inside yourself and inspire enough insight to make you evaluate your life. At times, their interpretations were so mingled with self-evaluation, I could not tell where the book left off and the student began. When Anna read Danielle Steel's *Daddy*, about a woman who puts her own needs on hold until her family's needs are met, she wrote:

Sarah was a writer, and soon after she and Ollie got married she accidentally got pregnant. Sarah was so upset, thinking I want to continue my career. On the other hand Ollie was thrilled to death. Sarah finally excepted her pregnancy. They eventually had two more children and when the kids got older, Sarah had to much free time. She started thinking about how success[ful] everyone was except for herself. She decided she wanted to go away to college (Harvard). She needed to do something for herself. Everything she did was for her husband and children.

I could see this happening to me. I married young and he's older. I could have rushed into having children. I do want a family. But I decided I needed to go to college first. I might not even work when I'm done with school, but I want to find out more about what I want before I get locked in.

Lucy was most impressed with the sisterly love described in *The Color Purple*, and she too applied the message of the book to her own life when she wrote, "This novel showed me that I should cherish the times that I have with my sisters now and tell them that I love them (even if sometimes they get on all my nerves) we all need each other because one day we are going to move our separate ways." Vivian also read *The Color Purple*, and took away a similar message with which to inform her life. "You better thank God when the people around you show their love freely. You think about what it means to live with contempt like Celie did. Lots of people do. I'm going to remember this when my mother gets smothering. She just loves me." After reading and reporting Joseph Valacchi's statement that he wished he could live his life over again, Jerry wrote, "I wish I could go back to my high school years and instead of sleeping and being silly I would have worked and gave 110%. But I can't, so, I will have to deal with it. Yet it will haunt me a long time. There are no time machines." These self-revelations, and the resolutions that often came with them, had nothing to do with comprehension, as we reading teachers understand it, and these were throwaway comments as far as literary criticism is concerned, but these books—a bestseller, a Pulitzer prize winner, and a work of nonfiction—went to work on my students, just as they went to work on their books. "To read and to understand." Have we even begun to scratch the surface of what this means?

I like strong opinions, strongly expressed, even when I loathe the values behind them. So I love to see my students express themselves with certainty in response to the social and political ills about which they read. When Rebecca read Kozol's *Rachel and Her Children*, she wrote, "I don't believe in my opinion that President Regen was in fault alone for the way Welfare was cut for these poor people," which was Kozol's ax to grind. Like Sara though, as she struggled to understand apartheid, Rebecca grew frustrated by how little she felt she knew about politics. She later wrote, "It don't make sense but this book [*Rachel and her Children*] makes it sound like the goverment really don't care that people are poor and can't get ahead. I am maybe not understanding but it seems like Jonathon Kozol is saying that they want some people to be poor. I can't figure out how that helps the economy though." Trust me, Rebecca, you are not alone. About *The Valacchi Papers*, Jerry wrote, "I feel organized crime should be dealt with a lot harder. Because if they would have dealt with Valacchi on his first arrest harder then I feel he might have been a different person. But instead they give minimum sentences so the person thinks that it must not have been a bad crime." In recent years, I have listened to the canonization of Rush Limbaugh because of his book *The Way Things Are*, and I know that in the months ahead Howard Stern's *Body Parts*, bound to be a huge success in workshop, will elicit praise of *this* self-serving hate monger's worldview. My motto is love the thinker even if you hate the thought.

I have learned to ask students to speculate about the lives of their characters by asking what happens after the last chapter. It was students in that first class who taught me to encourage this kind of interpretation. I mean, talk about "continued processing." After reading the Toni Cade Bambara short story "The Lesson," Lucy speculated—without prompting from me—about the future of the main character, a child named Sylvia. "She will listen and learn and not think she knows everything. She becomes sensitive and caring. She starts to take school seriously and does well. Instead of using her anger and boldness negatively she uses it positively and is respected by many people. Sylvia in my opinion would be a great attorney." Jerry wondered how Joseph Valacchi's life would have been different if he had faced more consequences for his early crimes. "At first I thought he would've straightened up. But then I was thinking that maybe all he was good at maybe was being a thug. He did'nt want to have to earn anything the hard way. So I can't just see him driving a cab or being a teacher."

While all my students made use of the various interpretive avenues I have described, each one had strong preferences for finding his or her way home. Lucy was a heavy hitter when it came to figuring out the psychological explanation for why the characters in her books acted the way they did. What indeed does happen to a dream deferred? Jerry, a great believer in fate, tended to examine the meaning of his books philosophically. He wanted to see how people dealt with the slings and arrows life threw their way. Anna used her own life as a litmus test for what rang true in the books she read. Mac too saw the treacheries of his own young life reflected in novels. Ray was swift to pass judgment about who was in the right and who was in the wrong. Kelly wanted to set the record straight for the misunderstood. Rebecca and Sara wanted to understand homelessness and apartheid in some sort of big-picture political context.

What I learned from systematically scrutinizing these literary letters was that students drew upon whatever resources were at hand—their knowledge of politics, pop psychology, personal experience, values and beliefs—to interpret or to explain what they read and what it meant to them. At least this is what happened when I left them alone. I assigned no short essay questions like those found in college reading textbooks, so I did not determine what got discussed and how. These letters were not the formal explications of literature classrooms, which discourage the "maybe, maybe, maybe" these students fell back on to express themselves while acknowledging room for self-doubt. I was not checking their comprehension or their compliance, since both were assured. What I really think is that these letters let me look at how my readers made meaning in as close to a natural state as I was likely to get in an academic setting.

I understood what I saw transpiring through Rosenblatt's transactional theory, which describes a "linguistic-experiential reservoir" from which readers select both the public and private meanings they associate with the words found on a page, as well as the vast range of social, cultural, ideational, and personal experiences that created these meanings (1989, 159). I got a glimpse of how these readers, when left to their own devices, siphoned that linguistic-experiential reservoir in order to make sense of what they read. Lucy used her knowledge of popular psychology to explain Celie's transformation from victim to seer in *The Color Purple*. Jerry did not believe people could change. He thought fate was a done deal, a card dealt at birth, and this belief shaped his understanding of what he read. Ray felt contempt for those who made decisions based on what might anger their gods, yet he applied his personal and highly integral code of conduct to the actions of those he read about. Mac, with an empathy that was almost a sixth sense, expressed and understood the pain his characters would have felt had they been real.

When we talk about the "prior knowledge" students need in order to understand what they read, what we have generally meant is *text-based* prior knowledge, in other words, knowledge presupposed by the words on the page. If a writer were to make a reference to the year 1066, for example, one of William Bennet's (remember him?) favorite examples of American adolescent ignorance, the reader would be expected to provide information about another William, the one who conquered England. If the reader cannot cough up that bit of information, he or she "misses" the point. But that kind of thinking presumes there is only one point, that which the words are thought to make. We have premised college reading around this idea of the one and only point. Witness the fact that we can test for it so convincingly. But my students reminded me that they brought enormous prior knowledge to their reading, whether it was Lucy's pop Freudianism or Jerry's fatalism, that the text may or may not have presupposed, required, or even anticipated. And, as a number of other interesting studies concur, they also brought beliefs, attitudes, and emotions that shaped their responses to literature (take a look at Dorfman 1985; Sadoski and Goetz 1985; and Sadoski, Goetz, and Kasinger 1988, for example). They might not have understood these books in the way a comprehension test would have asked them to, nor in the way literary critics might have, but these students brought bountiful information to their reading and summoned these resources to put together personally significant and perfectly plausible meanings. Just what is the field of college reading to make of that?

Talking About Reading

Reading was more than a ripple on the surface of our lives that semester. Overworked and still dazed by the new demands of college, these students found a place for reading in their lives, and we talked about it in our literary letters. My students learned that reading a book helped pass the time on the graveyard shift or in a doctor's office. We were readers who cranked up some soothing Metallica and curled up with a book at night. We read on the bus, in the bathtub, and we tried to keep one hand on the book and the other on the fork as we did what Dave called "read and feed." I confessed in my letters that the real reason I ate Thai and Chinese food all the time was that it did not have to be cut up. I could devote one hand to my chopsticks and the other to turning pages. We ordered our kids out of the room so we could read, and when our significant others wanted to discuss "the relationship," we said, "Not *now*. I'm reading." We stayed up too late, trying to finish one more chapter, and we talked about all these new discoveries as if we were the first persons on the planet to have read a book.

My students did and still do love the self-knowledge that comes from giving some thought to their reading preferences. That first class, I slapped together some by-now-well-worn overheads for a minilesson that detailed several elements of Marie Carbo's *Reading Style Inventory Manual* (1981), such as the ideal environmental, physical, and social stimuli for a person's reading. Carbo asks whether readers prefer silence or sound while they read, bright or dim light, eating or drinking, among other things. Students tell me that they have never given much thought to these matters, and they test their own preferences with the same zeal that somehow persuaded Pierre

Curie to expose himself to radiation, just to see if it would make his skin fall off. At the moment, Kyle is reading by candlelight to add a "gothic touch" to Edgar Allen Poe. Suzy is reading with, and without, a beer buzz to determine what works best for her. Okay, okay, so Marie Carbo may not have had these kinds of reading preferences in mind, but who can resist an inquiring mind? Most of my charges stick to her no-nonsense questions about what works best for individual readers. "You know," Dave wrote, "maybe I go to sleep every time I read because I lay down on my bed to do most of my reading." After describing a lecture from his composition instructor about how he should not try to read or write when he was playing his stereo, Ray wrote, "At home, the only way I can get enough quiet to read is to make more noise than everybody else in the house. There are nine kids still at home." Anna had a suggestion for me regarding her reading process: "You have to stay on me. I just don't take the time to read. But this is very important to me." Valerie wrote, "When I put the baby down for his nap all I want to do is sleep but I've been reading instead. That's about an hour a day I've added. I've been reading to him too like you said. I don't know what he's getting but I liked The Snowy Day."

We also sounded like readers when we made connections between the books we read. As I studied the students' letters, I could see their knowledge growing as they began to realize that what had seemed random was actually highly patterned. Dave wrote, "I've read two horror books now. Tell me why I get so tense when I know that good will whip evil's ass? Nobody'd read these things if the good guys did'nt win. But the books are still intense." After reading five teen romances in quick succession, Hiroko wrote, "In these books, the girl wind up with the right guy in spite of herself. She want the bad apple at first but the nice guy waits. She is hurt and then there is this friend who also loves her. Vivian told me this was bullshit and I should read The Color Purple." Valerie, sore at me for her growing addiction to V. C. Andrews wrote, "If a girl falls in love with a boy in one of her books you can bet money he turns out to be her brother except nobody knows cause they was sold at birth or something." Once my students began to understand formula fiction, my secret was out. They had marveled at my ability to predict the endings of their books, but they learned for themselves that I was not psychic after all, just experienced.

Since many of my students' reading preferences were pretty much hot off the presses, it amused me that they spoke with such conviction about their likes and dislikes. "I really like science fiction," Jackie said after completing her first science fiction novel, "So my next book will be science fiction too." Sara wrote, "The reason I didn't like that last book was because it was about two sixteen year old twins. I hate to read stories about people younger than me. The books that are about people who are already in college [have] much [more] reality to them than those about younger teens. So I will read one of those. Can you suggest one?" Sometimes these reading preferences stemmed from other interests the students had. Lance wrote, "Can I talk to you about majoring in history? I could read these books about the frontier for the rest of my life. I like writing to you about them too. I would like writing papers for a history class I think." Ray read Henry Miller's *Death of a Salesman* and Jason Miller's *That Championship Season* before writing, "Everybody thinks I'm gonna have a job w[h]ere my shirt has my name on it. But I read plays because I always wanted to try acting."

Like any readers, these students ran into trouble with their books. Despite my assurance that it was okay to bail out, they often persisted with particular books when, at first glance, it looked like they were in over their heads. When reading *Their Eyes Were Watching God*, Vivian reported:

At first it was very difficult for me to read. I could not understand the dialect in this story. So as I was reading every sentence I had to go back and say it out loud and sort of translate so I could understand it. At first I was going to drop the book. But the more I continued to read the more understanding I got.

Mac discussed his problem with *All Quiet on the Western Front*, as well as how he solved it, in consecutive letters. First he wrote, "I can't imagine what it was like being in the world war. What country they were in or how old they are and even keeping the characters straight. So I'm going to see the movie. Its on video." His next letter began, "The movie really helped. Now I can picture everything right. I see it in my head when I read now. I think its going faster too."

When it came to obstacles in their overall development as readers, these students also took a long look at themselves and set about solving their problems. Joanie wrote, "I don't know that much about what I like so I think I should read a variety of things to find out." At the beginning of the semester, Lance sounded a little more desperate, "I've got to find books that are really really good or I'm not going to pass because I won't read. This has happened before. I need to spend more time looking than some people." Other students had to solve reading problems that had nothing to do with what they were reading. You might remember that Ray's nuclear unit included nine siblings, of whom he was the oldest. He shared a bedroom with three of his brothers and found it hard to read when "one of them is whining, another is screaming, and the third one is punching the other two." But he wrote about one of his solutions: "Everybody clears out [of the house] on Sunday morning to go to church naturally. Instead of sleeping til noon I been getting up at ten and reading for an hour." Holly had a dilemma I could relate to, since much of my gruesome workshop reading simply could not occur if I did not have a home security system loud and aggressive enough to stop an intruder's heart (not to mention mine, should it ever go off). She wrote, "Well I can't read this book at night cause it scares me so bad I can't sleep. So I read when I get home from school before my mom goes to work. Then I'm not alone in the house."

Students used their letters to tell me about how they thought their reading was improving. Mac wrote, "I'm able to read for an hour at a time now without drifting off." Rick noted, "since I've been reading along with the [audio]tape I'm reading faster and I understand more." Joanie monitored herself very closely all semester, keeping a running record of what she had read in the inside cover of her notebook and how many literary letters she had exchanged and with whom. In her next-to-last letter to me, she wrote: "I told myself I would read seven books one every two weeks, but I just finished my nineth and we have a week left. I did better than I thought I could and I really liked every book I read." Ray wrote, "You don't know this but I started Cujo when you did and *I* finished first and you read like a speed freak." After she had finished Walker's *The Color Purple*, Lucy mentioned that she had read it before. "The last time I read it I was a sophomore in high school. The teacher talked to us a lot about what it meant, but I did not get very much out of it. But this time I got more out of the book than when I read it the first time. Like why is the title The Color Purple and how it was the women who made each other strong."

I was not surprised to find that my students rarely disliked what they were reading. I mean really, if a book was not to their liking, all they had to do was close it. When a book did let them down, it usually was because the ending "sucked" (i.e., was ambiguous or unhappy). Otherwise, they were having big fun and told me about it. "My first two books were okay," Lance wrote, "but The Frontiersman is great. I think about it all the time. Have you ever read a book before that you wanted to live in?" Holly wrote, "I'm starting to realize how fun reading is or can be. I wasted alot of years there." Valerie wrote, "I'm sleepy all the time with the baby but I got into this book so bad I stayed up until 1:30 am last night finishing it but it was worth it. Guess what time the baby woke me up? 2 am!"

Students spoke about the important people in their lives, and how these folks were reacting to their reading. Holly wrote, "My mom and grandparents have said they can't believe that I'm reading books for a change." Jackie wrote about a friend, an avid reader, who helped her find books.

"I'm going over to Bridget's tonight. She'll give me some ideas for what to read next. She found [the last book] for me. Her mom reads all the time too." Mimi also made use of the readers around her to locate good books, "I just finished a book a friend loaned me. You know her. She was in your class last fall. Katie Stevens." Jerry had less help. He wrote, "I told my dad I thought I was getting an A in reading and he said, so what you ought to be able to read anyway. The only thing I ever saw him read was the sports page in the paper." Lee-Ann's reading also met with less understanding; she wrote, "Last night my mom asked me if there wasn't something that needed done when I was reading in the livingroom. I folded the baby's laundry then went up to my room to read. I finished Dear Sister." Dave became the reader in his circle of friends: "I got my buddy Pete to read Fear and Loathing. He said it was the coolest book he ever read. Fucker was lying though cause its the only book he ever read. Steve's gonna read it next. What else did this guy write?" I ran into Dave, with his friend Pete in tow, at a street festival a couple of years ago. He introduced me to Pete as the teacher who had turned him on to Thompson, then asked me if I had read Thompson's piece about Clarence Thomas in a recent issue of *RollingStone*. What do you know?

Chapter 6

Dirty Laundry

Such a look. Mary Anne Pitman, the queen of qualitative research methods at the University of Cincinnati, has this look that suggests she must have heard you wrong because you surely would not have said anything so stupid in her presence. All I had said was that I wanted to do teacher research for my dissertation.

"You can't study your own students and your own teaching objectively."

We had been discussing whether or not she would serve on my dissertation committee. I was pretty sure the answer had been burned onto my retinas in the bare three seconds that I had been able to maintain eye contact with "the look." But we began debating, with Mary Anne mostly winning, and she apparently decided to see what I might do with my post-something-or-other ideas about objectivity and subjectivity. I left her office knowing that her take-no-prisoners approach to sound research would mean that to convince her, I would really have to convince myself first. Otherwise, the odds were so in her favor that I would be packing my bags to go study literacy in some place that did not having working toilets and hot water, like the public schools.

In traditional qualitative research, only those with no emotional investment in the events being observed can describe them "objectively," which is meant to mean "accurately." But someone this detached only tells part of the story. I have done research in other teachers' classrooms and have found myself going home, notes in hand, thinking, "Damn, he

balled that lesson up. Bet he doesn't sleep a wink tonight." So
what attracts me to teacher research is that I do care about
my students and my teaching, and I think that emotional
stake is part of the story my study needs to tell. My lack of
detachment as a teacher researcher does not allow me to separate the knowledge of a failed technique from the pain of
that failure. When I am up all night, readers of my research
are going to hear about it. And when it looks like I am doing
something right, well, tee hee hee. And one thing an outside
researcher cannot do that I will is show you how I corrected
the mistakes I saw myself make with that first class.

When It Was Truly Bad

I was brought up to believe that asking people direct questions
was nearly as ill mannered as smoking while walking, chewing
gum in public, or telling people what you really thought. Folks,
it was reasoned, would tell you what you ought to know when
they thought you ought to know it, and in the meantime, you
could always ask one of their neighbors. But as with so many
of my childhood lessons, it looks like I ignored this one. The
way I was most likely to respond to *anything* a student said in
a letter was to write back with a question calling for a literal
answer. I have spent most of my professional life jumping up
and down about the field's fixation with literal questions. How
many times have I argued that literal questions give students a
distorted view of reading, since recalling informationettes, like
what type of car Paul Sheldon drove in *Misery*, is not the point
of reading a novel? Yet we suggest that it is every time we give
one of our dumb compliance quizzes. And in nonfiction, what
happens to a reader's understanding of the whole text when
teachers or tests direct her attention to random bits of information? Think about that passage in the Nelson-Denny that
asks the name of Elizabeth Barrett Browning's dog (1981,
Form E, 5). What kind of reading is this? It is Tuesday, and

since Saturday, I have read two novels. You could put a gun to my head and I could not tell you the names of the main characters of either book if it meant saving my life, but I can tell you that Isabel Allende's novel *The Infinite Plan*, one of those books, is about a diaspora of the self, a modern Psyche coming undone and trying to put himself back together when there are too many pieces to coherently fit together. What matters more? So, even though I knew better, I spent most of my time asking questions like the one I posed to Lance about S. E. Hinton's *Rumble Fish*. In response to his thoughtful discussion of what fighting meant to Rusty-James and why he vowed to give it up but could not then live up to his own resolutions, I asked "How old was Rusty-James at the time of the fight?" Lance had the sense not to bother with answering. I think, or at least I hope, that I was just trying to make small talk with these literal questions, but we have to work harder than that. Otherwise, we run the risk of communicating to students that trivia is what counts when it comes to reading.

When I was not asking students literal questions, I seemed to be praising them for something or other. Here are a few examples of what I praised and how I praised it: "Your understanding of the book was good" or "I thought your interpretation of Sylvia's feelings was great." Well, first of all, since I had not read most of the books those first students wrote to me about, how in the world would I know whether their comments were good, bad, or indifferent? What I was responding to, I am certain, was how well they seemed to be supporting their views. That sounds legit, given the old regime of writing to the teacher as evaluator, but literary letters were supposed to be different. They were supposed to be a place where we could talk about books the way readers do, not the way teachers and students usually do. I had hoped that these letters would be written *to* me rather than *for* me, but I positioned myself as The One Who Knew What Was Good. Sure, I was mostly trying to be encouraging by lavishing a teacher's praise, but what I have learned since is that one good thought deserves another. What I mean is that the way to acknowledge a good idea is to engage it. I still find myself starting to write "what a good understanding you had" in my literary letters, but now I hit the delete key and rephrase. Today, a couple of weeks into a new semester, I wrote the following comment to a student whose ability to get below the surface impressed me:

> Your observation that <u>Natural Born Killers</u> is making a state-ment about how people have come to find violence so entertain-ing that they cheer for real killers (and yes, I also noticed Charles' "free O. J." t-shirt) made me think. I hate violence, but when Mickey killed the witness with a pencil, I loved it. Some-thing in me responded to his way of solving a problem. You cross Mickey or Mallory, they'll put a bullet through your freaking bad attitude brain. Most of the time, we just have to swallow it when we get dumped on. Your letter made me think about why it is we have started to cheer for the killers, as you pointed out. You do know, don't you, that this will be on my mind all day?

When I was not asking pointless questions or praising, what I was most likely to write in my letters to students was that I agreed with what they had to say about their books. Where did I get the nerve? Remember, I had not read most of the books for which I so boldly passed interpretive judg-ment. How could I disagree or even meaningfully agree? I made remarks like "I think you're right that . . ." or "I agree with your interpretation that. . . ." Yeah, sure, I was probably trying to build students' confidence, but why should their confidence in their reading have to be filtered through my yea or nay? And what worried me more was that I might be giving students the impression that it was important for read-ers to agree on meaning or that there was a right answer.

To be sure, there were and are moments when I am excited that a student and I have seen eye to eye on a book we have both read. Acknowledging affiliation is no crime. But I have learned to phrase this moment as a meeting of the minds, rather than as a granting of approval. This is how I responded to a letter from Penny, one of the students I met just two weeks ago, in which she discusses Terry McMillen's *Disappearing Acts*:

> You wrote that Franklin was everything that could go wrong with a man: he lies, cheats, drinks, lashes out, won't work, is always late, and lays all kinds of blame around. We sized him up in pretty much the same way. I think it's time for those three little words that mean so much in a relationship, "enough is enough."

Me and Penny, we thought we saw the color of that tiger's stripes, but who is to say that either of us is right? We just agree. Go and ask Cornel West or Ishmael Reed what they think of Terry McMillen's books.

Oh, and here was another of my favorite literary-letter activities: Putting Words in Students' Mouths. The following exchange with Lucy, about the Toni Cade Bambara story "The Lesson," shows you what I am getting at. Lucy: "When Sylvia began to realize what Mrs. Moore was try to teach her and the children she rejected it. She did not want Mrs. Moore to know that she understood what she was trying to teach them." Jeanne: "You're right that it was painful for Sylvia to learn that life is unfair and that there was an entire world of excessive luxury out there that she knew nothing about. She learned that rich people can buy *toys* that cost what it would take to feed her family for a year. Bambara captures that moment of insight, that lesson."

Lucy notes that Sylvia rejected the lesson, but she does not comment about what that lesson might be. Every classroom teacher must recognize this exchange from a typical classroom discussion. You think a student has missed the point or simply is not quite able to articulate it, or you just want to get somebody with some off-the-wall personal trip to STOP TALKING, but nice teachers do not come right out and say these things. So, you paraphrase the student's remark in such a way that you can shape it into a springboard for what you really want said. This is intellectual dishonesty—no stranger to me, one who will not tell students that much of what they enjoy reading puts her in fear for humanity—at its finest. But no student has ever called me on this. Maybe they are just used to teachers' acting this way.

Well, it was bound to happen. When I went back through these letters to analyze them, I discovered that on several occasions I had simply misread what a student had written. This was not subtle stuff either. Valerie's comments about a book called *Class Pictures* are as clear as a teetotaler's mind on Sunday morning:

> At the end of the story, the both of them are going away to college. Lolly is excited about going out on her own, but Pat isn't. Pat for many years has liked the principal at her old school. Even though he is now married and has a child on the way, Pat still doesn't realize what is going on. Before she leaves, she tells Mr. Evans of her feelings toward him. He in return reisures her that their would never be anything between them. She then faces this fact and goes off to college.

But they go right past me:

> So Pat is having a relationship with her high school principal? I guess, from what you wrote, that he returned her feelings. What do you think about that? Should a principal have a relationship with one of his students? I consider this sexual harassment, even if she consented, because there is unequal power between them. A young girl is no equal to a grown man, and this gives him the upper hand, and of course he has power over her school records.

What can I say? I had a point, just not the right one. You would think students would ask me to please get on the right page, but not once has a student ever mentioned the error of my ways. Maybe they are afraid to, since I am the teacher, but maybe they are taking pity. They have seen me acting witless before.

Something I did not do in that first round of literary letters was to write about the books I was reading, even when it was one a student had recommended to me. Maybe I just forgot or was too concerned with being responsive to the students, but

I knew I needed to do this and was surprised to learn that I rarely did. I have since mended my ways. When I talk about my books, I can "model" interpretation, talk about the reading problems I run into, and give students something to play off of as they compose their letters to me. If they can think of nothing else to say, they can always ask me about my book. I also introduce about fifteen new titles to a class just by reading and writing about them. The following excerpt is typical of what I generally write about whatever I'm reading:

> I'm still sticking with my goal of getting better acquainted with science fiction. I bought another of what they call "cyberpunk" novels, <u>Mona Lisa Overdrive,</u> because I liked the title. The future looks pretty grim in this book. One thing this author, William Gibson, seems to think is that we're going to run out of places to put our trash. The streets of the future he foresees are littered with used appliances and junk cars. The water and air are toxic, and so are most of the people. People scavenge what they can. And the gulf between the rich and the poor is absolute. There is no middle class. Most of the characters are what we would call "street people," but they're not depressed. This is just life as they know it. Makes me think we human beings can and will adapt to almost anything. That makes the book hopeful to me.
>
> All of the characters in the book are in some sort of trouble, and they're all in different parts of the world, but you get the idea early that they'll come together to get themselves out of their respective messes. Here are the characters: Angie, a star who hears voices in her head and dreams other people's dreams. Kami, a ten-year-old Japanese girl whose father is extremely rich and powerful and whose mother recently committed suicide. Sally/Molly is an assassin, businesswoman, and adventurer who, tough as she is, is still fond of the sad little Japanese girl. There's Slick Henry, a lost soul, and Gentry, a brilliant lunatic. And Mona, with a questionable past and more luck than sense. The story itself is almost impossible to follow, to tell you the truth, but I loved the characters. I have a soft spot for stories about unlikely people getting together to get out of a jam.

Let me add that when students and I have read the same book, the literary letters we exchange are less articulate in that our references are knowing rather than contextualized. I mention this because most of the examples in this book will not prepare you for how little sense the letters you and students write about a book you have both read will make to other readers. And, more important, even to you, if enough time has passed that you have forgotten many of the details about a particular book. There is something wonderfully fraternal about these letters that jump right in without much summary or introduction, something eager and touching and to the point. This sort of exchange did not occur before I allowed what I was reading or had read to become a subject of discussion. Here is a letter from Ellen, a current student who very much wanted to be included in this book, about the Olivia Goldsmith novel *Flavor of the Month*. I hounded Ellen to read the book, because I knew she would love its bitchy, twisted, and fun story. My comments in brackets fill in the missing information that Ellen assumed I would know. Her letter let me know we had seen eye to eye as readers.

Dear Jeanne,

I really like Flavor of the Month. At first I was apprehensive about the size of the book. But I was never tempted to put it down. Everything that Mary Jane put herself through [two years of dieting and cosmetic surgery to become "beautiful"]. And in the end to find out that it wasn't what she really wanted out of life. All the glamor and the glitter, sounds appealing but there's always the hard knocks in life, no matter what you do. I was glad when she got involved with Sam and he didn't know who she truly was [he had dumped Mary Jane for a prettier woman—before she had all her surgery]. And for him to think she would just sit back and take it again. I was glad when she left him high and dry, he definately deserved what he got.

Lila was to funny, I knew something was different about her, but I never expected her to be a man. The Puppet Mistress [Lila's Hollywood star mother] was really sick and twisted. Can you imagine doing that to a little boy [making him dress, live, and act female]? I thought Lila's mom was cruel but that was the icing on the cake. No wonder she was so secretive, I can't even begin to imagine.

Poor Marty, he really got shit kicked in his face [he married Lila simply because she was beautiful, and he let her call the shots so he could keep her, and therefore never learned she was a he—fun book, I am telling you]. One thing for sure, Lila really did deserve that Emmy after all.

Sharleen was so simple but so wierd [but a great beauty who starred in a hit TV show with the transformed Mary Jane and the transvestite Lila]. I can't imagine, don't want to imagine sleeping with my own brother. Even though in the end Dean turned out not to be her brother. All those years she thought he was. [Reading between the lines? Ellen thought this was as sick as I did. Kinship is thicker than blood ties. Woody Allen should listen up.]

Dobe was a good guy, he really took care of them both [Dobe was the guardian angel for this pair who hit the big time].

And the way he got rid of their mom [by having a friend pose as a cop before she could spill the beans to the press about the dual nature of their relationship] was really a surprise. I never saw it coming. Well, I'm anxious to get started on my new book, so I'm going to close.

See Ya,
Ellen

Getting It Right

Do you know what a blue moon is? Yeah, me neither, but it makes for great country songs and, about as often as one is rumored to come around, I noticed that I was doing something right in these letters. I want to run these things by you, but I am not trying to develop a list of responses teachers should always include in their letters. You have to watch out for sounding stale or too calculated in literary letters. I have internalized these ideas I will describe, but there is no list I consult as I write. Instead, I do my best to go thoughtfully with the flow, follow the *tao*, and pay attention to what students are signaling they are ready to learn. For me to be able to relinquish control like this and to follow someone else's lead, since it goes against my training and my nature, means that I have to abandon any sort of plan. What I must have for my own peace of mind, however, are a few tricks up my sleeve —a few tried-and-true means of motivating a stalled reader, generating interest in a book, or coaxing the reluctant out of the shallow end of the pool. Take what you can use and leave the rest.

Smoke and mirrors, part one. Paul Ellis gave me the idea for what I call "previewing" when he handed me a copy of Pat Barker's *Blow Your House Down* and said, "You've got to read this book. It has the single most disgusting paragraph I have ever read. You'll know it when you see it." Naturally, I read the book with single-minded purpose and in mere hours. I did in fact know which paragraph Paul meant when I came to it, and I had to call him up to thank him for the nightmare. I wondered if my students would also be compelled along in their reading by these literary come-ons, and I learned that they were. Dave began reading *Misery* right after I had finished it, and when he reported that he was starting to get bored, I wrote, "My neighbors were out cutting weeds with a chainsaw the other day. The god's truth. But that's nothing compared to what Annie can do with a lawnmower. You're gonna flip when you get to that part." A week later, Dave responded, "That was so sick. I had to read it to a friend of mine. He says Koontz is better than King but I said top this." The fall of 1994, the big tease was about *Natural Born Killers*: "Mickey may not know how to read or write," I would say, "but wait 'til you see what he can do with a pencil." Any sentence that begins, "I can't wait until you get to the part where" seems to get students through a slump, as well as giving them something to talk about.

Another approach to getting or keeping students interested in a book is by dishing on its author. Once I learned that S. E. Hinton was a woman, not a man, as Lance and I had both assumed, I was on the wire to him. "This dude's a chick, Lance. So what, was she a teenage boy in a past life? We've been going on and on about how well 'he' knows what it's like to be a young guy. Go figure." When Jerry read a collection of cases put together by a famous criminal lawyer, I told him how my father, before he retired from the Justice Department, had had to work with this litigator and referred to him as an "insufferable prick." I ratted on a writer I met at the University of Iowa who could not keep his hand hands to himself when I was there considering if that was the place to do my MFA (it was not). When Lucy read *The Color Purple*, I showed her my signed first edition and gave it to her to keep. I wrote to Vivian, when she read *Going to Meet the Man*, and told her about the night some friends and I spent drinking in a bar called Kaufman's with the late James Baldwin. Go to readings and signings to collect stories for your students, and do whatever it takes to get students to these events. I say this even as I am losing my mind trying to get fifteen students organized and funded for a weekend trip to the University of Kentucky next week to hear Isabel Allende, Julia Alvarez, Carolyn Forché, June Jordan, and Paula Gunn Allen. At this moment, however, if I hear one more word about who cannot possibly stand to sleep in the same room with whom, I might just give them the keys to the university van and tell them to send a postcard.

When it comes to encouraging my students to run with the big dogs, that is to say take a risk, use their highly evolved minds, and think about what they read, I have discovered a few tricks that I like and they cannot seem to resist. One of my favorite things to do is ask them to speculate about what will happen to their characters after the end of the book. Now, you have to be careful to make sure students understand what you are asking. When I wrote to Mac about his book *Dear Sister* and asked what he thought the twins, Jessica and Elizabeth, might choose as their careers later in life, he answered, "I'm sorry but I forgot to tell you Jeanne. This is a made up story. The twins aren't real people so I don't know their careers." But when I am more clear with students about what I am asking them to do, I get an answer. This is what Lucy, after reading *The Color Purple*, speculated about the future of the main character, Celie:

> Celie will make things the rest of her life with her sister Nettie. More pants, and friends, maybe poems or stories about her life. She will use the talents that was held down. Its like how she learned to use her heart. Her old woman years are gonna be better than most peoples whole life. I wish I knew her.

As you know from Chapter 2, I do a minilesson on how we can predict what will happen next in our books based on our knowledge of form, language, and what kinds of stories make the bestseller list. Given what we know about prediction as an aspect of strategic reading—that it requires students to read actively, marshall textual evidence and linguistic knowledge, and keep putting the pieces together—I ask students to predict all the time. And actually, this is a way of getting at meaning that most students internalize pretty quickly, so I do not even have to ask them what they think will happen next. Literary letters, unlike just about every other writing-about-reading activity, lend themselves to prediction because they are written during the reading, instead of after the fact, when the chances for prediction are gone with the wind. Just as Valerie started the sequel to the V. C. Andrews novel *Heaven*, I asked her what she predicted this book would hold in store for the children. She wrote back:

> Well, I think the doll her mother left Heaven will have significance in the story. She'll learn more about her mother because of it. And the clothes in the suitcase from her mother, you know she'll wear those at some point. Why else are they in the book? And she'll look like her mother in them and that might convince her mother's rich family of who she is. As sick as Jane is all the time she will probably die. I couldn't even guess what will happen to Fanny except she probably will end up pregnant.

One thing I did not do enough of in those first letters but am much more likely to do now is challenge the content of students' books. I was overly cautious with that first bunch of students, because I thought they were more fragile than they really were. I thought they might mistake my skepticism toward the author as lack of faith in their critical ability. I am still cautious, but reviewing exchanges like the following one with Kim, made me realize the value of *intellectual* fighting words. Ruffle their feathers once in awhile. It keeps life interesting. Kim wrote:

> One of the things this book [*Wealth Without Risk*] talks about is never use life insurance as an investment, and boy do I know that for a fact! About a few years ago we had insurance policies on us (life insurance) and somehow we got roped into trying this other company out, well to make a long story short, we made a mistake, which cost us some money. Well anyway, he [author Charles J. Givens] says that instead of buying whole life insurance you should consider term insurance instead, which is what we just got. I tell you I'm finding myself comparing notes with this book. I'm always looking up our records of things to compare with his. Another type of insurance I've learned more about is the loan insurance. I always wondered about that. This is not a good deal. This only pays the balance of a loan at the time the insured dies. Say your car costs $12,000 and you die only owing 1 payment of $327, the insurance pays only that amount. I'm not trusting insurance companies again. They would never tell you all these things. It would cost their business, so now I don't have to depend on their honesty, I'll know just as much as they know and maybe more.

I answered:

> Well, I agree that life insurance is a poor investment, but who buys insurance as an investment anyway? What insurance companies sell is peace of mind. That's what you get for your money. Could it be that Givens is knocking down a straw man? That's an expression that means his argument is based on tearing down an opposing argument that no one would argue about in the first place. What do you think? What does Givens have to gain from convincing readers that they're being ripped off but he has answers for them?

Kim fired off a response the same day she received my letter: "You've been brainwashed by the insurance industry. They make you think you need peace of mind. What you need is coverage for what really might happen not what your afraid will happen. I don't want to see you taken advantage of. Will you at least read this chapter?" Maybe Kim has a point. As it happened, my then significant other was a member of the insurance industry who wished all existing copies of *Wealth Without Risk* would spontaneously combust. I did read the chapter, as Kim requested, but I still have whole life insurance.

I think the field's focus on comprehension (understanding) rather than interpretation (explaining) has gotten us in the bad habit of approaching every text, even novels, as fact-finding missions. This hit home for me when I read Louise Rosenblatt's "Language, Literature, and Values," in which she describes coming across an assignment asking students to tell what facts they had learned from a poem (1985, 71). So I try to remember to ask students how books made them feel and to discuss my own "affective responses" as well. When Lucy was reading the Alice Walker short story "How Did I Get Away with Killing the Biggest Lawyer in the State?" I asked her how she felt when she read the scene in which the main character kills the lawyer who has been ruining her life. Lucy answered, "I wanted to kill him myself but I was shock when she went and did it. Murder just is not the answer. I was upset with her." I remember one day in class last spring when a student on one side of the room was weeping over the ending of Kaye Gibbon's *A Virtuous Woman* and another was laughing over Jerry Seinfeld's *SeinLanguage*. Not too many days later, I was reading the parody *The Ditches of Edison County* in class and lost it, tears came to my eyes I was laughing so hard, and the students called time out and insisted I read the book aloud. We laugh when we read, we mutter under our breath, we get mad, and a book can put us in a lousy mood. Why not talk about this stuff in reading class?

One last thought along these lines. I think it is important to answer every question a student asks me. It is simple courtesy and it also signals that students can engage us every bit as much as we hope to engage them. Dave led me to an insight about my own history as a writer when he asked, "You said you read Fear and Loathing in college. I bet you loved it. Did you want to write like him?" I replied:

> You're right. I did love the book in college. I wanted to be a writer, and I thought he lived the way writers had to: Edge City. He was a risk taker, playing with guns, and drugs, and alcohol. Hemingway lived like that. Lillian Hellman, one of my favorite writers, spent about thirty years of her life drunk and getting thrown out of good restaurants. I honestly thought that's what writers had to do to have experiences worth writing about. But you know, Hellman wrote well in spite of the way she lived, not because of it. And Thompson just kept writing the same book over and over. It's a funny book though, life on the ultra wild side.

If It Walks Like a Duck

At my dissertation defense, one of my committee members suggested that I revise to avoid using the verb *to teach*, since that connoted the kind of direct and directive instruction I was trying to reduce in my own work. Well, I prefer to redefine the verb rather than replace it. I am a teacher, and I really like the sound of those four words. And there is a time and a place for direct instruction in literary letters as well. The difference is that I was not the one who mapped out what students should learn; instead, they let *me* know. When the students turned their attention to discussions of themselves as readers, I responded as an expert. There were some beliefs and values about reading that I hoped to cultivate, as well as some misconceptions I wanted to clear up. For example, Anna voiced her concern about how she "drifted away" while she was reading. I wrote back:

> Have you ever wondered if "drifting away" is a good thing, particularly when you read a novel? Maybe the <u>book</u> sent you off on

the daydream. It takes me forever to read an author named Margaret Atwood because her books make me think about things that have happened to me, or how I envy how well she writes. Just a thought.

Anna did not get back to me on that one. And really, since our field does not know whether to pull out the garlic or to say a prayer when it comes to the spooky elements of reading, why should Anna take it on? Louise Rosenblatt writes about the reveries books evoke in readers, and Donald Murray (1986) went way out on a limb with his "ghost text" business, but all in all, we ignore students when they tell us that they dream about the characters in a book or just cannot stop thinking about an old friend as they read. Reading stories conjures up the stories in us. But this is just one of those aspects of reading that we avoid as teachers and researchers because we do not know how to count or to measure or to evaluate it.

Lucy wrote to admit that she was actually rereading *The Color Purple*, since she had been assigned to read it in high school. Although she wrote that she was getting more out of the book this time around, her real concern seemed to be that I would think she was cheating because she had read the book before. Where do they get these ideas? I had to set the record straight right away:

> Rereading books is a great idea. For one thing, you learn a lot about yourself as a reader, especially how much more you pick up on as the years go by. You're older, you know more, you read better. What seems important one year may take second place to another part the next time you read a book. Now that I've read The Temple of My Familiar, Walker's next novel, I want to reread The Color Purple because some of the same characters turn up in the second book. I'll know things about them that weren't even in the first book. And now I've seen the movie, so I'll picture everything differently (snow in Georgia? Right!). The meaning isn't just there in the words, unchanging. The meaning you get from a book changes as you change. Isn't that great?

When Jerry wrote that he was getting a little bored by *Man Is the Prey*, a book entirely devoted to different animals that are known to kill humans, I wrote back, "Jerry, you don't have to read every chapter. So far, you thought sharks and hyenas were cool, but elephants were boring. You could just read the chapters you're interested in." He responded, "But does it count as a book you've read if you only read parts of it?" I answered, "Doing what pleases you as a reader, whether it's abandoning a book or skipping chapters, is not cheating. You are in charge." I have to say that a hundred times a semester, since my students have been convinced that really reading a book means reading every word. I know they are less able to skip and skim than I am, since I have greater linguistic and literary knowledge, but they seem to have been so indoctrinated by the idea that reading must somehow "count," and that they are accountable to a teacher, that this is a battle I have failed to win. But if all you want to know about Magic Johnson's life is how he coped with his HIV diagnosis, why bother to read the rest of the book, unless you enjoy delaying gratification? If you decided to read Pat Conroy's *Prince of Tides* because you wanted to see how your (you hope more ethical) therapist compared with the psychotherapist in that book, why not read only the parts devoted to their sessions? No matter what I say, I think my students still expect some sort of a quiz. I seem to be taking on a reading ethic that failed to get them to read what they were assigned in high school but also failed to teach them to at least please themselves.

Students wrote (and still write) about the difficulty of working reading, a new activity, into their already busy lives. They want my advice, since they sense that I have a very full schedule and still manage to work hours of reading into every week. I am realistic enough to know that telling them to take a sledge-hammer to their television sets is an idea that will not fly, so I try to work around the aliterate or antiliterate structure of their lives. Jerry wrote, "I like to read in the kitchen because the light is good. But every time the old man comes in for a beer he wants to know what I'm doing just sitting there. I tell you

Jeanne it makes me sick." I wrote back, "Go down to Value City and buy yourself a lamp for ten bucks. Put it in your room and read there. If you want to make a point with Pops, go for it, but if you want to read, retreat to your room." LeeAnn, a recent mother, struggled with her new role and wrote about it in her literary letters. "My mom is still mad at me about the baby. If I want to do anything else like read my book she starts cutting her eyes at me." I wrote back, "You could try reading your books to the baby. He'll get what he needs, language and physical contact with you, your mother will see you taking care of the baby, and you'll get to read your book while keeping everybody else happy." Vivian wrote, "You don't have kids, do you? You know, I can't even go to the bathroom alone. If I go down to the den to read well this is when somebody decides she's finally going to do her chores and starts running the sweeper. If I want to talk to my kids all I have to do is pick up a book. Do you have a minilesson on kids?" I wrote back:

> You're right. I don't have kids. I'm pretty out of touch, huh? Can you make them move out? I guess not. How about laying down the law? Say, from 7 to 9 in the evening you do schoolwork, no interruptions, no exceptions? Are they old enough to leave alone? What if you were to go to your public library or some other quiet place to do your reading? I haven't been there, like you say, so I'm not full of ideas. Why don't you do a minilesson? We have four mothers in the class, and you could invite people to share their strategies. [She did, and I still use the minilesson, although it is less convincing in my hands.]

When I think about it, I try to undo some of the beliefs my students have absorbed about reading. And remember, this is the same voodoo I used to teach. Anna was critical of herself for not looking up every new word she encountered, and I had a flashback to the days when I asked students to circle "unknown vocabulary words" in red ink. When I wrote back to her, I was writing to the hundreds of students I had messed with on this matter:

What would it do to the flow of your reading if you were to stop and look up words all the time? If you don't look up the words but are able to understand the passage anyway, then it probably means you've figured out the meaning of the word from the context in which it is used. If a word interests you, by all means look it up and learn about it, but I don't think you're reading sloppily because you get the gist of a word without knowing the dictionary definition. If an unknown word completely trips you up, then looking it up is one way to recover, but it's not poor reading to keep going when you are understanding well enough.

Joanie wrote about an ACT preparation book that she read outside class. "On the parts where you read passages and answer questions the book said to always read the questions first. I never do that. No wonder I don't do well on tests." How many times had this bit of lore come out of my mouth? Yes, Joanie, I read this advice somewhere as well, but I never stopped to think that there is no bit of advice that works for each and every reader. I wrote back:

> I'm not so sure about that advice to read the questions first. For some people, having the words of the question floating around in their heads, or trying to read for only the answers, could cause problems with their comprehension. If the book has some sample tests, why don't you try it both ways. Read the questions first on one test, then read the passages first on another test, and see which seems to work best for you.

To "Teach" Workshop

If you ask me, these letters were collaborative, in the positive rather than treasonable sense of the word. While students called the tunes, this was a dance in which no one led exclusively and no one always followed, but somehow we avoided crashing into other couples or stomping all over one another's toes. We had to invent literary letters as we went, and this meant we were not locked into our steps; instead, we had to pay useful attention to one another and to improvise. I think I respond to students' letters in a way that is more consistent with my theory now than I did then. I know too that I backslide, get lazy or busy, and write inane comments like "I'm glad to hear you're enjoying your book." Like I am going to be *unhappy* to hear this? I should have challenged students more in those first letters, and I still wish more students would challenge me, at least by saying I have misread their letters or that I am putting words in their mouth. And maybe I am being intellectually dishonest when I do not voice my concerns about the violent nature of much of our reading. But then, to avoid the risk of silencing one another, perhaps some things just have to be left unsaid.

I give a lot of thought to how students perceive me in their letters. They cuss, admit when they are bored or confused, and tell me if they cannot seem to make themselves read outside class. They report their triumphs. They tease me, urge me to read their books, give me advice about their classmates, and tell jokes. My final judgment is that my students see me as collaborator, witness, and consultant. We are in collaboration when it comes to the invitation I issue, which is for them to find the rewards, if any, reading might hold for them. My job is to be a partner in this pursuit by recommending books, paying attention to what students say about what they read, and trying to ask compelling questions to help them find out just how much they think and know.

My second role in these letters is as witness. I think students write to me as someone who can *attest to what has taken place*. Think about how totally gratifying it would be to have someone around who really knew how hard you work. I did this for students in our letter exchange. Think of Lance, when he wrote, "I hardly know where to begin. The last two weeks I've read more than I think I ever have," or Holly's comment, "Well, I've finished another book! Wow! That's three." With these weekly letters, I am never far away from being in the right place at the right time for a student to say, "Look, Ma, no hands." Response journals are episodic in most cases; students write regularly, but we only collect them every two or three weeks. But students decide when it is time to write a literary letter to me, and so I am aware of their triumphs almost *as they occur* (and just think about the implications of a move to e-mail). Literary letters let me get so close to the action, in spite of the chaos of having eighteen students reading eighteen different books at any given time, that I can be this witness that all of us would dearly love to have.

I mentioned a consultant role as well. During those moments when I was called on to teach—or at least to know *something*, since I was in charge—my role was quite different from that of any other teaching experience I have had. Instead of determining what students should learn, when they should learn it, and if they had learned it, I was on call. Although I did not get to the phone in time on more than one occasion, and sometimes it looked like I was asleep when I answered, the way these letters worked was that I had to be ready to teach when the opportunity arose, not just when I saw fit. I never knew what the day's letters would bring, and I had to be opportunistic, seeing lessons where they lay. "Leading [or teaching] from behind" has become a cliché in the whole language movement. Okay, I confess, I have always joked about it, comparing it to the enigma of the sound of one hand clapping. Which is what, a slap? So what is leading from behind? A shove? These letters put me in the unfamiliar and ambiguous position of not being totally in charge. I could no more predict the day's demands than I could line up the semester's minilessons like ducks in a row, because I never had much advance warning about what the students would want or need to know. What I have finally concluded, though, is that all this "leading from behind" business really means is teaching what someone tells you he or she wants to learn.

And what of students? What were their roles in these letter exchanges? Well, they were collaborators and consultants as well. I set events in motion by insisting that everyone read, but students took it from there. They updated me on their progress and their plans, as any partner would, but they did not seem to be filling me in to get my approval; rather, they were letting me know where we stood, how we were doing. And when a student, your collaborator, is not pulling his or her weight, you know it. Believe me, I have received some vapid, blah-blah letters in the years I have been doing workshop. In fact, one of my favorite students and best readers this semester writes the emptiest letters I have ever read. And the pure hell is that this student writes at least twice a week because she likes me too. I stare at her letters, struggling to find something worth commenting on, something I can work into a conversation. If even five percent of student letters fell into this category, I think I might go back to multiple choice. Oh, and let me ask, how many times have my students looked at a letter from me and heaved a similar sigh? We all have mindless moments.

As consultants, these students told me about their reading. They told me things a standardized diagnostic test never could, such as how difficult it is to read when your children are setting fire to one another or when your younger siblings are reenacting the war between the states just because somebody called someone a "dumbass." From what I hear, there are books students want to read but do not want their peers to know about. And from time to time, students leave books on the cart between classes to avoid taking them home and running the risk of troubling their parents' or their partner's mind (for example, *The Erotic Silence of the American Wife*). I have learned what a nuisance a point-of-view shift can be, as well as how confusing it is when an author starts getting artsy with chronology. These and subsequent students have recommended books to me, introducing me to the scores of authors and titles that have become my workshop library. And when I have asked for direct help, they have not refused me, whether I have asked them to write to a way-weird classmate or to pick on someone their own size if they are feeling like crap about how they read. And maybe they have been my witnesses as well. It had been a long time since I felt I had something useful to offer my students as readers.

We teachers have to develop a voice in our literary letters. I struggled with it, rejecting the way I handed out facile praise and treated agreeing with a student as something worth talking about. In *In the Middle* Nancie Atwell writes that she did not want to sound like a teacher's guide (1987, 170). I guess my last bit of advice is to find your own voice in these letter exchanges. It is not so important that you always remember to ask probing questions or that you constantly scan students' letters to identify one of their strengths to exploit. Students read these letters, but their success does not hinge on whether we have asked them to predict often enough, probably has little to do with us at all, in the long run. So, relax. Say *shit* every now and again so they know they can trust you. Tell jokes. Use bad grammar for emphasis. Pull their legs. Tell them what another student or a friend of yours had to say about the same book. Get so carried away about a book you are reading that you forget to ask about theirs. Whatever. All we have to do in literary letters is to ring true. That is the voice students want to hear.

𝒲 *Chapter* 7

Decision Time

*W*hile Carole Edelsky provided me with a theory that allowed me to peer into the dark night of a discipline clouded by two opposing teaching approaches, she also burdened me with some seriously value-laden language. The observation that certain types of reading are "inauthentic" implies that they are bastard or criminal, and those sound like fighting words. But much of the reading we encounter in school, as well as in the workplace and even in the day-to-day management of our lives, involves simulated reading. I can wish for a world in which no one ever had to read anything he or she did not feel personally inspired to digest, but given that I am an administrator who generates enough memos and reports to fill a new file drawer each year, I am reminded to be careful what I wish for. While I will stick with Edelsky's language for consistency, I do not want to imply that simulated reading is inferior to authentic reading. The problem is that, like Edelsky, I think that our field has confused the two, collapsing these two types of reading into a single phenomenon (1986, 178). If I were to come up with less judgmental descriptions of these two types of reading, I would call them "reading as it happens," when there are few constraints, and "the construct of reading," which we have created in order to systematically deliver instruction, assessment, and mass information.

So what if there really are two types of reading, that which is authentic and that which is simulated? Well, it would explain a few things. This theory that there are two types of reading, the real and its facsimile, also explains why the field is divided into two equally sincere but increasingly hostile pedagogical camps. Nowhere was this made more clear to me than at the December 1991 meeting of the American Reading Forum in Sarasota, Florida, in which some recreational games on the beach turned bitterly competitive when it became clear that our two teams had, quite unintentionally, divided by whole language or skills-oriented sympathies. Naturally, the whole language team won the events requiring collaborative effort, but of course the skills-oriented team won at water scrabble, all that work with letter recognition having paid off. Seriously though, that conference made me aware that I not only was running into a brick wall whenever I tried to talk to skills-oriented teachers, but I also turned to stone whenever they tried to talk to me.

I left that conference depressed by our total inability to find any common ground, when we all called ourselves reading educators. On the flight back, my colleagues and I speculated, rather hastily, that the advocates of skills approaches must not be readers themselves, because, as we saw it, they had no idea what reading was. But this is beginning to make sense to me now. The reason we seemed to be speaking two different languages was that we were. Skills-oriented practitioners and whole language proponents all describe what they do as teaching reading, but we are actually teaching two different phenomena that have the same name. Skills-oriented practitioners teach "reading," the kinds of simulations with which students must come to terms if they are to do well in school. Those who embrace a whole language philosophy, on the other hand, are teaching authentic reading, that in which meaning construction is not inflexibly constrained by bureaucratic needs for assessment, evaluation, or uniformity.

Skills-oriented practitioners view reading as the acquisition of sequential skills, which begin with letter recognition, then sight-sound correspondences, then word recognition, and so on. In college reading courses, the approach is quite similar, really, since it entails teaching vocabulary words, clearly a decoding emphasis, and working with controlled texts, which are much like those basals first graders use. In college reading textbooks each reading passage is geared to teach a specific new skill, such as identifying the author's main idea, noting cause-effect relationships, distinguishing between rhetorical modes, or understanding paragraph organization. Edelsky explains why skills-oriented models make sense to their advocates:

> With the assumption that reading and writing consist of separate skills, it is a short jump to the idea that the exercise of any one of the skills in seeming isolation also counts as reading or writing. My claim, on the other hand, is that separate reading/writing skills do not add up to reading or writing, that the use of some sub-part of the whole activity outside of the whole activity may have no relationship to doing that sub-activity within the whole activity. (1986, 173)

Edelsky goes on to say teachers, researchers, legislators, and the public, who "equate tests of 'reading' and 'writing' with authentic reading and writing, not only believe instruction in 'reading' and 'writing' leads to reading and writing, but . . . actually prefer the inauthentic to the authentic" (179). Skills practitioners *intentionally* teach simulated reading, although they would bristle at having it called that, because their emphasis is on teaching students how to tolerate and to manage school-based reading, which requires them to focus on referential meanings, to arrive at single answers, and to suspend their private understandings and their personal needs and preferences as readers because these might interfere with correct comprehension, compliance, or both. When real reading is given any consideration at all, the fragile assumption is that once students learn to "read," which is the hard part, real reading should take care of itself.

   Kenneth Goodman calls whole language "an attempt to get back to the basics in the real sense of that word—to set aside basals, workbooks, and tests, and to return to inviting kids to learn to read and write by reading and writing real stuff" (1986, 38). The belief behind this is that literacy develops as a response to personal and social needs, such as getting family finances in order or learning about romance or experiencing the thrill of suspense without encountering any actual danger. Whole language proponents understand that when we outlaw private meanings or neglect to let students develop their own purposes for reading, we are banishing critical qualities that make reading authentic. Also central to a whole language philosophy is the conviction that reading is a process of constructing meaning rather than decoding or comprehending. The important question to ask students about their reading is not whether they circled the right answer but whether what they read was meaningful. Judith Newman flat out says, "As teachers, we must keep in mind that it is the students themselves who must construct meaning. No two individuals reading the same passage will arrive at exactly the same interpretation" (1985a, 109). Whole language, Newman says, also promotes student choice as essential to literacy learning (1985b, 5). Even when we cannot allow for total choice, our assignments need to be flexible enough to allow students to discover their own purposes for the reading, upon which our pedagogical intentions can then hitch a ride. Within the whole language movement, I think there is a shared belief that if students become readers first, then simulated reading poses few demands they cannot master if they want to. I suspect this is true, but it takes a luxury college reading teachers do not have: time.

Do skills practitioners really prefer inauthentic to authentic reading, as Edelsky suggests (1986, 179)? Ouch. But I have another take on this. I do think it is far easier to teach subskills, which gives the impression that we know what we are doing, than to acknowledge that experience is the only teacher when it comes to constructing meaning, the badge of authentic reading. Skills practitioners are looking for shortcuts, ways to deliver instruction quickly and efficiently that will teach the majority of kids to comprehend what they have to read in school. Teaching authentic reading, on the other hand, is labor-intensive and time-consuming, unless our students have been born into critically literate households. We have to model meaning construction, and we have to listen to summaries of teen romances until we either gag or our readers decide it is time to move on. We have to sit still as our students read Stephen King novels, all the while knowing that the next semester they are going to have to tackle psychology textbooks. When you look at a classroom of college developmental reading students, you are looking at folks who are running out of time. What college skills-oriented approaches have done is to prioritize. The thinking is that these students had to be ready to read biology textbooks yesterday, and so the emphasis is on teaching them the presumed rudiments of understanding academic reading, which entails coping with texts in which the pragmatic constraints of "objective" information delivery interfere with reasonable readerly demands such as voice, relevance, and interest. Basically, we have to do something, we have to do it fast, and these are the sorts of things the field has chosen to do.

Now, my job, as I understand it, is supposed to be helping students shore up their "reading" in order to prepare them for college, but I am not doing that, not directly at any rate, because I am teaching authentic reading instead. As a hostile colleague of mine likes to jab, reading about teen love or the mayhem of a Stephen King will just do wonders for my students when they have to read up on adolescent development or abnormal psych. I fully acknowledge that my approach is not going to have students ready to handle all the reading they will face in college. I offer students very little in the way of direct help with mastering the simulated reading that lies ahead, and I know it. While I believe that if reading becomes normal, routine, and even moderately pleasant in its associations, students will be more able to read for another's purpose or to read texts they find uninteresting or irrelevant, the fact is that my students and I truly are just about out of time.

As things stand now, my options are pretty limited. I can keep teaching real reading as if there were no tomorrow, or I can put together a typical simulated reading course. We can get out our highlighters and underline those main ideas until either the pages become saturated or the paragraph makes sense, whichever comes first. I can adopt one of the newer college reading textbooks, one with a reading-across-the-disciplines approach, which provide excerpts from college biology, psychology, history, or sociology textbooks and comprehension exercises, and the students and I can then occupy ourselves with simulations of simulated reading. But, I have to tell you, I am not even slightly convinced that pursuing a skills-oriented approach will make my students masters of simulated reading. There just is so little evidence to support the idea that teaching simulated reading actually enables simulated reading. And if, as I theorize in Chapter 5, what these learners have rejected about reading in the first place is the simulated reading we teach in school, then what will I accomplish by giving them more of the same? They still may remain non-"readers," and they may not have the chance workshop provides to discover the pleasures of authentic reading. Teaching real reading is something I now know I can do. And I believe that getting students to read their heads off is the only way they can become fluent in both reading and "reading." So, with regard to real reading, I have to ask, if not now, when?

The pressure is more acute for college teachers, since our students are in the court of last resort, but all reading teachers are in the same bind. We want our students to be avid readers, so that they will continue reading and learning for a lifetime, but instilling a reading ethos into our classrooms requires consistency, persistence, and time to let students find their own ways to enter reading. We also know that our colleagues in other disciplines expect us to teach students to complete the kinds of simulated reading they assign. And of course the tests are hanging over our heads. American students are not reading so well these days? Well, just pass some legislation that says they have to read better, that should do it. Real reading does not stand a chance under the enormous pressure to teach students how to do well on "reading" tests. So if we want to teach reading, rather than deadening simulations, what are we to do?

First, we have to get our own house in order. We have to put an end to the wholesale confusion between "reading" and reading. Skills-oriented practitioners and whole language teachers are at one another's throats because we simply have no conception of how the other guy can buy into such different means to the same end. But our goals *are not* the same. We need to be sinking our teeth into each other about just what kind of reading it is we should be teaching. And to sort this out, we need to look at where our beliefs about reading, as well as our curriculum guides, come from. Researchers, theorists, publishers, legislators, and colleges of education have built an empire out of simulated reading. To abandon it now would be to render many people's careers pointless, because the paradigms of reading and "reading" are mutually irrelevant. Textbook publishers and test designers would have to scramble to redirect their energies into developing materials that would be useful for teaching and evaluating real reading. "Reading" researchers would have to learn how to study a type of reading that defied quantification. Legislators would have to get the message that stomping their feet will not improve how our students read. And yes, many teachers will have to let go of what has worked in the past to redefine what it means for reading instruction to "work."

Blowing down the house of "reading" has to happen from the bottom up. Whole language, a grass-roots movement based on what teachers have learned about reading from paying attention to their students, has already started huffing and puffing. Whole language is driven not by the nation's need for reassuring, if hollow, assessments or legislators' need for accountability or empiricists' need for quantification; rather, it is a philosophy built on the needs of individual learners and teachers' knowledge of the real reading they endeavor to promote. If we want to teach reading, we can no longer count on the knowledge handed to us by the "reading" establishment.

We need to participate in knowledge making within our field, through teacher research, and look to the theorists and researchers who have taken what we have learned and pushed it to its esoteric extremes. If we need more training, we should get it. If we need more courage to subvert curriculums we do not believe in, then we should network. If we doubt that tests of simulated reading tell us anything useful about our students, then we have to challenge them, not only when the results reflect poorly on our readers or our instructional practices, but when they are favorable as well. And we need to demand that our colleagues in other disciplines start making themselves useful.

Where is it written that academic reading has to be inauthentic? Why are our colleagues persisting in their overreliance on textbooks, from first grade through college, when there are so many outstanding books written for interested nonspecialists from which they could choose? We use textbooks because they are comprehensive and reasonably objective, yet the writing is usually voiceless. Textbooks, though organized to aid recall, contain few passages that are memorable. If all one reads in school are pages of factual information that must be recalled, in contrast to pages that are experienced as affecting and indelible, then the pragmatic constraints of information delivery interfere with authentic and aesthetic reading. Instead of caving in to pressure to teach our students to "read," why not encourage our colleagues to make real reading the foundation of their courses?

Bringing about change means taking risks. Why "fix" instructional approaches that many people do not feel are broken? Why would any of us plunge into the unknowns of teaching real reading when it produces such ambiguity, anxiety, and a reduction of our control? Upheaval is only one of the many difficulties ahead. We will have to do more reading and thinking. We will have to talk ourselves blue in the face to convince our colleagues, as well as our superiors, that there are new developments in reading that they need to listen to. The only thing that makes it worthwhile to start pushing this rock uphill is that it is far worse to feel that what you are teaching students actually interferes with their reading or is a poor substitute for what you know reading might mean to them if they had another chance. You know it when you get there.

Appendix A: Course Syllabus for LAP 091: Reading Workshop

> *My education was the liberty I had to read indiscriminately and all the time, with my eyes hanging out.*
>
> — Dylan Thomas

Reading Workshop

The purpose of reading workshop is to help you make reading a regular part of your life. The more you read, the better you read. The only way to improve your reading is to read **a lot.** What you read doesn't have to be hard or boring or deep. It's the practice you rack up that counts. So, I want you to read books that are fun, that hold your interest, and that you can get through quickly. The thing about reading is that you never "peak." The more you read, and the more years you spend reading, the better you get. There really are no shortcuts, it just takes practice, and I want you to find great books that make practice pleasant.

Reading workshop begins with a minilesson, which is then followed by a status-of-the-class check-in. For the remainder of the class, we will either read our books or write literary letters.

Workshop Participation

For each day you attend class and follow the guidelines listed below, you'll receive five points. If you miss class or fail to participate, you won't get credit for that day. Here's the deal:

1. You must read or write literary letters for the entire period.

2. You can't do homework or read material for another course.
3. You must read from a book.
4. You may not talk or disturb others.

There will be 32 days of reading workshop for which you can receive credit, at 5 points per day. This provides a total of 160 points. Workshop participation counts as 1/3 of your final grade. You must have a minimum of 130 participation points to pass the course, regardless of your performance in other graded categories.

145–160 points   = A (95%) (0–3 absences)
140 points   = B (85%) (4 absences)
135 points   = C (75%) (5 absences)
130 points   = D (65%) (6 absences)
125 points (or below) = **automatic course failure**

Literary Letters

Literary letters are a means for us to discuss what you have been reading. You'll write to me, and I'll answer. And you'll write to your classmates, and they'll write back to you. These aren't book reports, and I don't want you to write lengthy plot summaries. I just want you to tell me about your book and your reading, in general. I'll discuss these letters in more detail during the second week of class, but I'll state the guidelines here:

1. During the semester, you must write 12 letters to classmates.
2. During the semester, you must write 12 letters to me.
3. Letters should be no less than one page, single-spaced, in length.

Your literary letters count as 1/3 of your final grade. You receive credit for any letter you sign your name to. In other words, it doesn't matter if you are writing to someone, or answering a letter he or she sent you. Literary letters are graded on a pass/fail basis:

24 letters   = pass (95%)
23 or fewer letters = fail (0%)

Goals Setting and Evaluation

In negotiation with me, you will set personal goals for yourself as a reader. Maybe you want to read a long book or read something different from what you're used to or find a favorite author. At the beginning of the second or third week of class, I'll give you a set of potential goals to help you think about what you want or need to do as a reader. Then we'll have a conference in which we discuss and decide on your goals.

At the end of the semester, I'll ask you to evaluate honestly your progress in achieving your goals. I'll write back with my own honest observations about your progress. Your goals count as 1/3 of your final grade. This portion of your grade is determined subjectively, but you have the opportunity to assess and to explain your own progress.

A = 95%
B = 85%
C = 75%
D = 65%
F = 0%

Final Grade

A = 95 – 100%
B = 85 – 94%
C = 75 – 84%
D = 65 – 74%
64% or below = course failure

Materials

1. You need a pocket folder in which to keep your literary letters.
2. Since the course requires no text but does provide you with books to borrow, each student is expected to contribute $10 to sustain and enlarge the class library. If you purchase a book to read, and then donate it to the class library, you'll be reimbursed from the class library fund. I'll also purchase books, at your request, with money from the class library fund.

Appendix B: Minilessons

Strategies for Selecting Books (from Students' Reading Inventories [Atwell 1987])
Improving Reading (from Students' Reading Inventories)
Improving Reading Through Practice
Authentic Versus Inauthentic Reading
Writing Literary Letters
Managing the Letter Exchange
Oral Reading
Process: Social Settings for Reading
Process: Environmental Settings for Reading
Process: Emotional Settings for Reading
Text: Independent, Instructional, and Frustration
Abandoning Books
Models of Reading: Data-driven
Models of Reading: Interactive
Models of Reading: Transactive
Reading Fiction: The Fictional Curve
Reading Fiction: Point of View
Reading Fiction: Chronology
Reading Fiction: Suspending Disbelief
Making Meaning Vs. Comprehension
Prediction: Word Level
Prediction: Sentence Level
Prediction: Text Level
Setting Reading Goals
Speed Reading: The Big Lie
Reading Poetry: Line Breaks
Reading Poetry: Metaphor and Image
The Role of Prior Knowledge in Reading
Strategies: Getting Prior Knowledge in a Hurry
Metacognition: Recognizing Strengths and Weaknesses
Metacognition: Monitoring Comprehension

Politics of Meaning: Who Decides What It Means?
Politics of Meaning: Banned Books
Politics of Meaning: Censorship
Politics of Meaning: Textbooks
Critical Reading: Propaganda
Critical Reading: Bias
Critical Reading: Persuasion
Critical Reading: Point of View
Critical Reading: Don't Believe Everything You Read
Strategies: Reading When You Have Kids
Reading to Children
Oral Reading: Children's Literature
Book Awards: NBA, Pulitzer, Nobel Prize
Signed Copy Show and Tell
Building Home Libraries
Recommendation Roulette (A Game)
Reading Textbooks: Motivation
Reading Textbooks: Understanding and Remembering
Strategies: When You Just Don't Know What It Means
Strategies: Keep Reading!
Writing Your Self-Evaluation Letter

Appendix C: Some Suggestions for a Class Library

Horror

John Saul	*Guardian*
Stephen King	*Carrie*
	Misery
	Pet Semetary
	Gerald's Game
	It
	The Stand
	Christine
	Thinner
	Salem's Lot
Anne Rice	*Interview with the Vampire*
	The Vampire Lestat
	The Queen of the Damned
	The Tale of the Body Thief
	The Witching Hour
	Lasher
Bram Stoker	*Dracula*
Dean R. Koontz	*Lightning*
	Midnight
	Watchers
	Dragon Tears
Jay Ansom	*The Amityville Horror*

Suspense/Thriller

Joy Fielding	*See Jane Run*
	Life Penalty
	Night Woman

Nancy Price	*Sleeping with the Enemy*
Thomas Harris	*The Silence of the Lambs* *Red Dragon*
John Grisham	*A Time to Kill* *Pelican Brief* *The Firm* *The Client* *The Chamber*
Michael Crichton	*Congo* *A Case of Need* *Jurassic Park* *Rising Sun* *Disclosure*

Romance/Glamor

Jude Devereaux	*A Knight in Shining Armor* *The Taming* *Twin of Ice* *Twin of Fire* *Sweetbriar*
Danielle Steel	*Accident* *Vanished* *Daddy* *Changes*
Olivia Goldsmith	*First Wives Club* *Flavor of the Month*
William Nicholson/ Leonore Fleischer	*Shadowlands*
Robert James Waller	*The Bridges of Madison County* *Slow Waltz at Cedar Bend* *Border Music*

Action/Adventure

S. D. Perry/   *Time Cop*
Mark Verheiden/
Mike Richardson

Dewey Gram/   *True Lies*
Duane Dell'Amico/
James Cameron

Alan Dean Foster/   *Alien*
Dan O'Bannon/
Ronald Shusett

John August/   *Natural Born Killers*
Jane Hamsher/
Quentin Tarantino/
David Veloz/
Richard Rutowski/
Oliver Stone

Frank Sacks/   *Extreme Justice*
Robert Boris

Richard Marcinko   *Rogue Warrior*

Bridge Books

Terry McMillen   *Disappearing Acts*
                      Mama
                      Waiting to Exhale

Dominick Dunne   *A Season in Purgatory*

Tom Wolfe   *Bonfire of the Vanities*

Truman Capote   *In Cold Blood*

Alice Walker   *The Color Purple*

Maya Angelou   *I Know Why the Caged Bird Sings*
                      Poems

Rosellen Brown   *Before and After*

Pat Barker   *Blow Your House Down*
                     Union Street

Sue Miller   *The Good Mother*

Kaye Gibbons   *Ellen Foster*
                     A Virtuous Woman
                     Charms for the Easy Life

Ellen Gilchrist   *I Cannot Get You Close Enough*
                     Victory Over Japan

Bibliography

Atwell, N. 1984. "Writing and Reading Literature from the Inside Out." *Language Arts* 61 (3): 240–52.

———. 1987. *In the Middle: Writing, Reading, and Learning with Adolescents.* Portsmouth, NH: Boynton/Cook.

Carbo, M. 1981. *Reading Style Inventory Manual.* Roslyn Heights, NY: Learning Research Associates.

Dorfman, M. 1985. "A Model for Understanding the Points of Stories: Evidence from Adult and Child Readers." Paper presented at the Seventh Annual Conference of the Cognitive Science Society, Irvine, California. ERIC, ED 335605.

Edelsky, C. 1986. *Writing in a Bilingual Program: Habia Una Vez.* Norwood, NJ: Ablex.

Goodman, K. 1986. *What's Whole in Whole Language?* Portsmouth, NH: Heinemann.

Goodman, K., and Y. Goodman. 1983. "Reading and Writing Relationships: Pragmatic Functions." *Language Arts* 60 (5): 590–99.

Henry, J. 1990. "Enriching Prior Knowledge: Enhancing Mature Literacy in Higher Education." *The Journal of Higher Education* 61 (4): 425–47.

Murray, D. 1986. "Reading While Writing." In *Only Connect: Uniting Reading and Writing,* ed. T. Newkirk, 59–86. Portsmouth, NH: Boynton/Cook.

National Assessment of Educational Progress. 1981. *Reading, Thinking, and Writing: Results from the 1979–1980 National Assessment of Reading and Literature.* Denver, CO: National Assessment of Educational Progress.

Newman, J. M. 1985a. "What About Reading?" In *Whole Language: Theory in Use,* ed. J. M. Newman, 99–110. Portsmouth, NH: Heinemann.

———. 1985b. Introduction to *Whole Language: Theory in Use,* ed. J. M. Newman, 1–6. Portsmouth, NH: Heinemann.

Paris, S. G., B. A. Wasik, and J. C. Turner. 1991. "The Development of Strategic Readers." In *Handbook of Reading Research,* vol. 2, ed. R. Barr, M. L. Kamil, P. Mosenthal, and P. D. Pearson, 609–40. New York: Longman.

Rosenblatt, L. M. 1938. *Literature as Exploration*. New York: Noble and Noble. Reprint, 1968.

———. 1978. *The Reader, the Text, the Poem: The Transactional Theory of Literary Work*. Carbondale, IL: Southern Illinois University Press.

———. 1985a. "Language, Literature, and Values." In *Language, Schooling, and Society*, ed. S. N. Tchudi, 64–80. Portsmouth, NH: Boynton/Cook.

———. 1985b. "The Transactional Theory of the Literary Work: Implications for Research." In *Researching Response to Literature and the Teaching of Literature: Points of Departure*, ed. C. R. Cooper, 33–53. Norwood, NJ: Ablex.

———. 1989. "Writing and Reading: The Transactional Theory." In *Reading and Writing Connections*, ed. J. M. Mason, 153–76. Boston: Allyn and Bacon.

Sadoski, M., and E. Goetz. 1985. "Relationships Between Affect, Imagery, and Importance Ratings for Segments of a Story." In *Issues in Literacy: A Research Perspective*, 34th Yearbook of the National Reading Conference, ed. J. Niles and R. Colik, 180–85. Rochester, NY: National Reading Conference.

Sadoski, M., E. Goetz, and S. Kasinger. 1988. "Imagination in Story Response: Relationships Between Imagery, Affect, and Structural Importance." *Reading Research Quarterly* 23 (3): 320–36.

Smith, F. 1983a. *Essays into Literacy: Selected Papers and Some Afterthoughts*. Portsmouth, NH: Heinemann.

———. 1983b. "Reading Like a Writer." *Language Arts* 60 (5): 558–67.

———. 1985. *Reading Without Nonsense*. New York: Teachers College Press.

———. 1986. *Understanding Reading: A Psycholinguistic Analysis of Reading and Learning to Read*. Hillsdale, NJ: Erlbaum.

Stahl, N. A., M. L. Simpson, and W. G. Brozo. 1988. "The Materials of College Reading Instruction: A Critical and Historical Perspective from 50 Years of Content Analysis Research." *Reading Research and Instruction* 27 (3): 16–34.

Staton, J., R. W. Shuy, J. K. Peyton, and L. Reed. 1988. *Dialogue Journal Communication: Classroom, Linguistic, Social, and Cognitive Views*. Norwood, NJ: Ablex.

Sternglass, M. S. 1986. "Writing Based on Reading." In *Convergences: Transactions in Reading and Writing*, ed. B. T. Petersen, 151–62. *Urbana, IL: National Council of Teachers of English.*

———. 1988. *The Presence of Thought: Introspective Accounts of Reading and Writing*. Norwood, NJ: Ablex.